LIVING
WITH
PICTURES

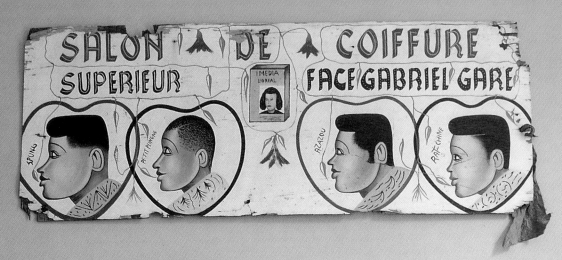

LIVING
WITH
PICTURES

ALAN POWERS

MITCHELL BEAZLEY

To William

LIVING WITH PICTURES
by Alan Powers

First published in Great Britain in 2000 by Mitchell Beazley,
an imprint of Octopus Publishing Group Ltd,
2–4 Heron Quays, London E14 4JP

Copyright © Octopus Publishing Group Ltd 2000

Executive Editor **Mark Fletcher**
Executive Art Editor **Vivienne Brar**
Project Editor **John Jervis**
Editor **Penny Warren**
Design **Lovelock & Co.**
Picture Research **Jo Walton**
Production **Nancy Roberts**
Proof reader **Sue Harper**
Index **Hilary Bird**

Artwork for pp.132–139 by **David Ashby**

ISBN 1 84000 243 3

A CIP record for this book is available from the British Library

Set in Stone Sans

Colour reproduction by ERAY SCAN PTE LTD, Singapore
Produced by Toppan Printing Co., (HK) Ltd
Printed and bound in China

CONTENTS

INTRODUCTION

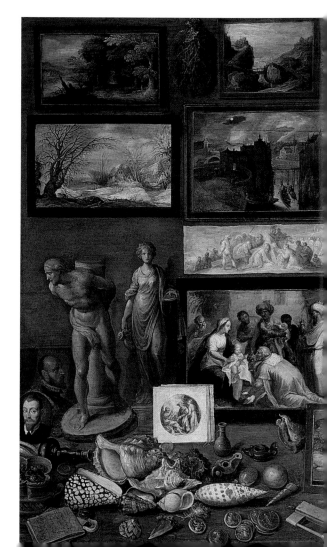

Left *Young Woman Standing at the Virginals* by Jan Vermeer (*c*.1670) shows precious paintings in a Dutch townhouse of the seventeenth century. The painted lid of the instrument illustrates a way of using painting on objects of furniture that was beginning to give way at this time to 'fine art' in its familiar form.

Below A cabinet painted by Frans Francken (1581–1642), with a variety of small framed paintings and drawings of different genres, as well as sculpture, shells and other curiosities. We still delight in making such arrangements now, though seldom as intensely crammed as this.

Hanging pictures on the walls of a home is one of the most stimulating ways of making decoration personal and meaningful. Most people have pictures, but often their effectiveness is diminished because of lack of knowledge about how to display them, or lack of the adventurous spirit that transforms picture-hanging into an art form of its own. However, these skills may be learned by looking at what others have done and by experimenting at home.

Pictures are too readily taken for granted in our image-saturated world – it is hard to remember quite how few pictures or images people saw in a lifetime, even as little as a hundred years ago. Colour printing of any kind was uncommon until relatively recently and most newspapers were solid with text. As a result, people must have devoured every image they came across, holding them in their memory. Eighteenth- and nineteenth-century peasants in Europe used to hoard woodcut images – religious, moral or satirical – that the pedlar brought to the door, pinning or pasting

them directly on the wall, while in Orthodox Christian countries every home had its icon, placed diagonally across the far corner of the big communal room, to be saluted on entry. These were pictures that were more than just commodities or interior decoration.

Higher up the social scale, images had many purposes. They could glorify ancestry, point out a moral, tell a story, stimulate an appetite for food or sex, bring a whiff of exoticism, or hold up an approving mirror to the existing state of things. Today, pictures have not ceased to fulfil such functions, and serve many more besides.

Some people like to surround themselves with densely hung walls, like a Renaissance princeling in his *Schatzkammer*, or treasure-chamber. Sir Winston Churchill's secretary, Edward Marsh, for example, was well known for hanging pictures on the back of his bathroom door when other places were taken up. Indeed, once picture-buying becomes a habit, it is hard to live any other way, and in this book you will find ways of using just about every sort of space, including the ceiling.

Above William Hogarth's opening scene from the series *Marriage A-la-mode* (1743) shows, amidst its moral lessons about the dangers of conspicuous wealth, a regular picture-hang, composed in pairs and groups of four, that combines canvases with elaborately framed and valuable looking-glasses.

More common today, however, is a minimalist look with very few pictures that are often abstract, and which in the right conditions can be calming and beautiful.

Modern communication is moving rapidly away from its bias towards the written word, and is making increasing use of non-verbal images and of the spoken word instead. A greater degree of sensitivity and skill in arranging our visual surroundings may be becoming more important as a result of this need for improved visual literacy in all areas of life.

Pictures are not just conveyors of information, however, but are the very things that establish the positive character of a room. Their capacity to create a mood and to influence what goes on around them through subject matter, colour or form is hard to quantify, and therefore tends to be discounted, but it is instantly recognizable in certain houses where pictures seem to be especially at home. Pictures make their contribution to rooms, and rooms can add to the special quality of pictures in return. This book looks at the excitement and potential that exist in this relationship.

Above The architect Serge Chermayeff designed this 1930s house for himself. The colour scheme was built around the abstract painting by John Piper, which was carefully selected to fill the end of the room. Some of the sliding wooden doors contained pictures which could be revealed as required.

Right Linley Sambourne House in London, an artist's home preserved from the 1870s. The upper line of the 'hang' is kept regular and there are approximate vertical columns of pictures, but no rigid order, giving an effect of rich multiple layers.

COLOUR, TEXTURE AND FORM

'Perhaps colour is impossible to talk about,' wrote the Scottish painter Alan Davie in 1961, 'Colour is like a scent indescribable; or like a chord struck on a harp in the darkness.' Colour, as he suggests, has the power to change our mood and affect our sense of well-being, yet its effects can never be entirely encapsulated in words.

Use of colour depends on many things. Each culture gets accustomed to certain colours that might seem out of place somewhere else. For example, people in tropical countries with very bright light tend to enjoy strong colours that would look strident in temperate places. Furthermore, what works for some individuals may not for others. Particularly in paint and textiles, it often seems safest to reduce the amount of colour: pastel shades keep their popularity even when fashion moves between pure white and strident limes and oranges or dark reds and greens.

In a home setting, a room decoration scheme may already be decided before it is known what pictures are going to hang there. However, if you have pictures already, it is worth taking into account their relationship with the colour scheme of the room. If a picture has a dominant colour, it is not usually best to pick up on this in the decoration, although a weaker version, modified with some other colour, or mixed with white to make a pastel, will often work successfully.

Above This corner comes alive with light, enhancing the strong blue-yellow contrast in the painting, which is a more intense version of the wall and textiles.

COLOUR

In achieving a satisfying colour harmony between pictures and decoration, a sense of structure is important. The walls can sometimes usefully take their cue from a picture, picking up on the major and minor colour themes in the work and responding with a mixture of similar and complementary colours.

It is now possible to buy paint to match thousands of shades, but it can be more satisfactory, if a little messy, to mix yours at home. Get some artists' paints, such as acrylics, and try different combinations. Manufactured paints tend to emphasize intensity of colour rather than the subtlety found in old paintwork which can make a really satisfying background for pictures. This may have been the result of imperfect materials or mixing, but what modern paints gain in consistency and uniformity they lose in liveliness and softness.

Rather like adding seasoning when cooking, it is possible to add different tints to improve both quality and depth in paint colour. It is often a good idea to put some black in the mixture, for example, to take the edge off the intensity of the dominant pigment. This will hardly alter the colour itself, but will make it a better background for pictures. A slight addition of the complementary colour is also often productive. Red is the complementary colour to green, orange to blue, yellow to purple, and so on. In addition, colours that lie between the primaries also have their complementaries, and colour theorists have constructed different diagrams to show these theoretical relationships. Some of the painter-decorators of the nineteenth century worked out elaborate rules for placing one colour next to another in a decorative scheme so that the whole room would hang together.

Left Red plastic chairs could spell danger in some situations, but here they are an effective foil to a varied assortment of pictures, balanced by the dark blue throw on the sofa.

Right Singing colours make a cheerful grouping of furniture, wall and pictures. The jug, although a small element, plays a crucial role in bringing it all together, acting as a microcosm of the other colours. The pictures are hung from a picture rail and the exposed strings, although generally not attractive, seem to work here because they are repeated and carefully matched with each other.

14

Some of these schemes have been preserved, others reconstructed in historic buildings, and they offer good scope for working out what the underlying principles were. Although we are unlikely now to paint our rooms with such elaborate and detailed schemes, it is worth discovering how colour has been understood historically, and what hidden potential it has.

One effective technique is to paint an undercoat on the walls in the complementary colour to the final colour you want, so that light passes through one colour to reflect off another. You can also tint the walls delicately with very diluted watercolour paint over the top of white, so that they are not coloured in the conventional sense, but acquire a sort of glow.

It is important to consider the specifics of the room. How much sun does it get, and at what time of day? Morning light is cooler than evening light and it may be wise to balance these qualities with decoration. For example, a north-facing room should not be too cold in colour, or too dark. Another consideration is whether the room will used more during daylight or under artificial light. If the latter, will it be lit for practical activities or to give a sense of atmosphere? Some pictures glow magnificently in semi-darkness, others may look lost or forlorn, while too much brightness around a picture can spoil the effect of its own inner colour and light.

Left The relationship of colour and form between these pictures makes them a strong pair, able to stand up to equally strong-minded furniture. The lights, which resemble a bunch of lilies, add a humorous touch.

Right The blue world of the picture draws the viewer in without any distractions in this setting which is as pure as an art gallery. The mottled marble of the fireplace corresponds to the texture in the centre of the painting, helping to unify picture and room.

Right There is a subtle formal match between the UFO-like building in the picture and the classic light by Paul Henningsen. The circular theme is taken up again in the chair backs and other details, making a mutually supportive group of shapes.

You may find that the artist has balanced the main colour in a composition with one or more complementary colours. You can respond by introducing modified versions of these colours into the room, using one for walls and another for the floor or curtains perhaps, or by choosing patterns that give you a ready-made oppositional mixture. Or you can let the picture do the work in making its statement against the room. Finally, if a picture has a dominant colour, you can take a risk and saturate the room with the same colour.

Today, there is so much choice of colour, both in terms of available materials and awareness of different cultural traditions, that many people prefer virtually to deny colour and turn to white minimalism. Their home environment will then be calm and contemplative, but this does not have to mean a complete denial of colour. There are many different kinds of white with different light-reflecting qualities, any of which might be appropriate to the mood of a particular space and the pictures that will be hung there. Grey, which has long been popular in French decoration, is an even more fascinating colour. It usually works best in a warm tone with plenty of red mixed into it and makes an excellent background for pictures, especially if the pictures themselves have a lot of white in them.

The quality of paint surface is a further consideration. The chalky, matt finish of old-fashioned distemper has acquired new converts at a time when emulsion paints dominate through their predictability and convenience, but look increasingly like the plastic material on which they are based. Lime wash is another traditional medium that can look very alluring in a modern setting because of its lively surface and, like distemper, can easily be tinted with the addition of artists' powder pigment mixed into a paste with water. Both tend to look feeble and transparent when first applied, but they become increasingly opaque as they dry, lightening in colour tone at the same time. These paints are most suitable for building up layers of colour on a wall, so that it can then reflect light with a real sense of vibrancy and depth.

Below The magazine rack may seem like an afterthought, but it echoes the sinuous lines of the painting to just the right extent in this gloriously coloured room where the rest of the furniture is so sturdy and solid.

TEXTURE

It may often seem secondary to colour in terms of how we see things, but texture is a key quality in decoration. Some pictures depend a lot on the texture of their surface: think for example of the thick *impasto* of certain oil paintings, or of a rough canvas barely covered by a thin layer of paint. Curiously, black-and-white photographs are particularly good at evoking texture, even though they have no actual texture of their own. There are works of art made from a variety of collage materials, some of which are chosen to give interesting texture contrasts, while smooth, highly finished paintings need something to give them contrasting texture, in much the same way that a salad needs a dressing.

Texture is often shown to best advantage when colour is most subdued. It works even more subtly than colour to connect the pictorial experience with our own knowledge of the world through the sense of touch as well as sight. Like colour, texture has a kind of musical scale, from rough to smooth, but with a more precise set of evocations. We can easily imagine being scratched by sharp thorns, abraded by sand, soothed by water or muffled by wool. These are qualities of texture that can be evoked through pictures and decoration, either by setting up similarities or by making contrasting statements about soft and hard, rough and smooth.

Above In these pictures made with gold leaf, it is hard to tell what is flat and what projects forward. The fruit may be a casual and transitory visitor to the scene, but it adds to the ambiguity by suggesting solidity.

Below The scraped, weathered texture of the painting, together with its forms and colours, is mirrored in the table and the lights, giving the picture a three-dimensional look, projecting it forwards into the room.

Opposite In this almost monochrome room, the sense of texture in everything is enhanced. The mysterious picture on the wall, with its illusion of weight and shadow, surprises you by being lightly pinned at the corners, emphasizing the lightness of its paper support.

Some works of art use texture in a primary way by incorporating the surfaces they wish to evoke, while others set out to create an illusion of texture – consider for example the still-life paintings of Chardin or the Dutch masters. As with evocations of colour, the artists seem to be trying to bring our eyes back to a realization of the extraordinary richness of the sensual world.

Even more than colour, a language of texture grows out of the things we have around us in our rooms. Designers, like the new generation of chefs, seem increasingly aware that our palates need to be tickled by different kinds of suggestion and so put us in touch with the experience of the natural world, especially, perhaps, in places far removed from the ocean or the countryside. Small objects in a room, like pebbles, shells or pine cones collected from a Mediterranean hillside, can alter the entire mood through their suggestion of texture.

There are also other ways of developing texture in a room. You could consider leaving brickwork exposed, stripping joinery or selecting characterful floor coverings, so that the sense of texture is sensed by the feet as well as by the eye and the hand.

Below *Impasto* is the term for oil paint thickly applied, as seen in the corner of this picture. The red beakers respond with their smoothness, setting up a colour match with a formal contrast.

Right The group of artworks has been chosen with a similar theme of box-like edges. Some of these edges belong to the works themselves, while the yellow square is actually a frame for a small photograph of a wicker ball. The visual geometric theme continues with the cube candle on the mantelpiece and the pure shape of the half-round pillow to the side of the fireplace.

The strong black rectangle frames the reproduction of a fresco of 1480–1 by Melozzo da Forlì, showing Pope Sixtus IV founding the Vatican Library. It might be too heavy in some settings, but it stands up to the strong competition from the decisive shapes of the chairs and the pure forms in this kitchen/dining room, where everything is smooth and shiny.

Below The forms of this simple black-and-white print echo the bathroom fittings. The gantry railings correspond to the gleaming plumbing, while the lifeboat and crescent moon relate to the twin discs of the mirror.

Right A large blown-up photograph of a succulent plant makes a compelling centrepiece in this carefully arranged room with its variety of natural shapes and strongly symmetrical layout.

Some older houses have plaster that is rougher than the highly finished modern product, and it is well worth leaving this as an exposed surface rather than covering it with lining paper, even when there are obvious areas that have been damaged and repaired. Slight variations and accidents in wall surface may look awful when the walls are bare but, as soon as you start to hang pictures, the texture of the blemishes turns them into positive assets.

A subsidiary aspect of texture is the awareness of fragility and hollowness. Glass objects introduce a quality of danger, quite unlike wood or wool, while stones placed next to glass seem to establish their own dialogue of solid and void.

FORM

Some pictures have very strong formal qualities. Imagine something that is neither highly coloured nor suggestive of texture, but still retains a visual structure with a strong sense of geometric composition, like a diagonal line or a circle. Pictures of this sort can be extremely effective in an interior. Rhythm acts as another kind of form: a series of pictures that repeat similar motifs establishes a strong sense of timed repetition in the viewer.

In rooms, form arises partly from what is there at the beginning, for example the shape of the windows, the proportion of the wall spaces, and the position of the doors. It then depends on what can be brought in to organize the form of the room. Pictures can make a big difference: those placed directly opposite windows or fire-places, or centred on their individual piece of wall, establish strong lines of connection and set up a grid-like structure for the room. It is common to work with imaginary horizontal lines, so that tops of pictures are lined up with each other and two or three rows hang one above another. Placing pictures high or low makes a considerable difference to the visual weight of the room. Since we are most often sitting down when looking at the pictures, it is a good idea to hang them lower than the height we expect when standing up, as this gives a more restful effect.

Left Use of a single colour range concentrates the eye on form. The careful off-centre placing of the picture enhances its own depiction of a strong shadow cast from the left, a motif that recurs in the fireplace itself. In the right-hand part of the room, the screen and the patterned ceramics set up another, quicker rhythm of repetitions, with contrasting horizontal and vertical lines.

Left An artful arrangement of picture and wooden objects intercepts the light and adds a feeling of three-dimensional depth. The contrast in scale between the upright carved tree-trunk and the little stool brings a quality of wit as well.

Above A mysteriously pure work of art is set among busy patterns on the wall, the chair and the chair back. Because of the close relationship of colour and tone among all the elements, the picture is improved by this contrasted setting.

Calm and order are not the only effects to aim at. Many pictures try to induce a sense of movement or directional tension which corresponds closely to similar effects that can be manipulated in a room. One could arrange a room to feel as if it were revolving, like a merry-go-round, although this would be impossible to live with. On the other hand, pyramidal structures of symmetrical and paired objects and images, such as are found around a classical fireplace, can be a bit stifling.

One of the great contributions of twentieth-century art was to emphasize the dancing quality of the visual world. The earliest abstract paintings of Kandinsky suggest this, as does Matisse's masterpiece *The Dance* (1911), painted when jazz was born in New Orleans. Later on, Jackson Pollock was inspired by his collection of jazz records to paint works alive with a network of oscillating movements. Apparently unstructured, these offer a kind of deep pool of form into which one can plunge, like a diver into water. Something of the same quality of movement can be the basis for a room.

There is also a middle way in which the underlying order is clearly apparent, but elements are deliberately introduced to subvert it; for example introducing asymmetry or placing furniture slightly off the grid makes the room look more friendly.

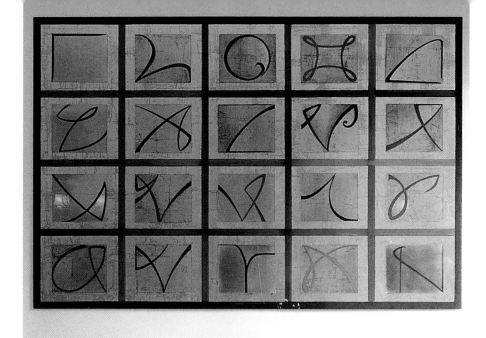

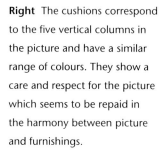

Right The cushions correspond to the five vertical columns in the picture and have a similar range of colours. They show a care and respect for the picture which seems to be repaid in the harmony between picture and furnishings.

MAKING ART FEEL AT HOME

Paintings, objects, prints, photographs and sculpture are not meant to be separated from ordinary life. Finding satisfying ways to incorporate them into the home is in itself as much a form of interpretation as writing books and articles about them. It calls on skills of visual organization that are not taught in schools. Perhaps this is because nobody thinks they matter, but they are immensely satisfying to develop for oneself. Even though there are no set rules, there are different ways of learning.

One should look at as many examples as possible, trying to work out what is going on visually, and remember successful effects. It is worth keeping a notebook for the purpose when visiting galleries, historic houses or museums. Photographs in books such as this one can be inspiring, but there is no substitute for a real, three-dimensional experience, and it is a pity that it is not normally possible to see new and innovative schemes of decoration in ordinary life. In addition, including art in the home is about experimenting, having the courage to make mistakes, and the energy to attempt something different.

The process flows both ways, so that a room can add to the significance of a picture as much as a picture adds to the significance of a room. Ideally, they should click together into a combination that seems natural and inevitable. When it works, there are few things more satisfying.

Right This traditional Japanese alcove has the shallow space and focused lighting of a stage set, with the scroll as the main player, and a basket of flowers essential to setting up a dramatic dialogue. The sparseness helps to create a meditative mood.

PRINTMAKING

PRINTS AND

A printed reproduction uses photography to copy the artist's original image onto printing plates. For an original print, the artist makes the image directly with one of the several printing media so that all the prints produced are equally 'original'. Relief printing is the easiest technique to understand. A raised surface is inked and pressed onto paper – rather like taking a fingerprint. Wood is a traditional medium for relief printing. The endgrain was used in the West as a fine medium that could be printed using the same presses as metal type. In the twentieth century, the work of artists such as Eric Gill led to a considerable revival of wood engraving on endgrain for book illustration and individual prints.

Etching and engraving using metal plates (also known as intaglio) dates from the Renaissance and was used to get a finer line tone. Some of Albrecht Dürer's most famous prints were made this way. The engraving technique is similar to that used on wood, but as the plate is printed from ink rubbed into the incised lines, these are dark instead of light. Etching produces lines on the plate by selectively exposing the drawn lines to acid which eats into the metal. The eighteenth-century Italian artist Giovanni Battista Piranesi pushed the capabilities of etching further than anyone

Above A nineteenth-century etcher inspects a print freshly pulled from the press. The copper plate lies on the bed of the press and passes through a heavy roller. Behind him is a leather ink pad for rubbing ink into the lines of the plate. This messy, physically direct form of printmaking continues to fascinate contemporary artists.

Left An etching workshop in the seventeenth century, when this technique was standard for illustrated books. The man at the back is inking a plate, while the one in the foreground uses the palm of his hand to 'bring up' areas of inking prior to putting the plate through the press.

Right Silkscreen printing at Curwen Chilford Studio, near Cambridge, England, a workshop offering professional facilities to artists. The coloured ink is pulled manually across the screen to make a small detail on the print.

Below A simple silkscreen poster from the 1980s, showing the value of this medium for flat pattern and blocks of colour. The image can be cut from a stencil or painted onto the screen with a liquid medium, or transferred photographically.

before him, even Rembrandt. Other techniques such as aquatint have been developed to achieve a greater range of tone. The artist Francisco Goya was among the first to use aquatint for his sinister and disturbing comments on life.

Lithography, invented at the end of the eighteenth century, was adopted for its spontaneity and freedom of touch by artists such as Henri Toulouse-Lautrec. Its prints can be identified by their crayon-like drawing or brushwork. More complicated to explain than relief or intaglio, it involves a grained surface, stone or metal plate that carries a printing image in a water-repellent medium. When the plate is damped, the ink adheres only to the image and a print can be taken. The ever-versatile Pablo Picasso invented a technique in the 1950s using a mixture of gouache paint and lighter fuel on the plate that produced a kind of textural mottling. Lithographs are often printed in colour from a series of plates, and can mimic the effect of painting.

Silkscreen, which is now technically highly versatile, is also widely favoured as a printmaking medium, requiring less specialized equipment than older techniques. Silkscreen used to be associated with flat colour, but in fact many textures can be achieved, and photographic images may be projected onto the screen, as famously used by Andy Warhol.

Prints by well-known artists are often good value. They will carry the artist's signature, together perhaps with the title of the print and a serial number showing the size of the edition, for example '3/25'. The letters A.P., meaning 'artist's proof', and H.C. (*hors de commerce*) mean they are identical to the rest of the edition, but were not originally offered for sale.

S till life is a genre of painting that takes domestic objects as its subject matter. According to classical theory, it stood on a level somewhere below landscape and portrait art – it was supposed to be easier to do compared with more elevated types of painting and it appealed to uneducated people. Despite starting with such a handicap, still life's directness and lack of rhetoric took it ahead of the rest of the pack as art entered the twentieth century, leaving the traditional hierarchy of genres turned on its head. In Cubism, painters concentrated on still life, finding through the genre a renewed sense of the poetry of everyday life with its guitars, café tables and newspapers.

Still life concentrates on the immediacy of experience, making the everyday seem miraculous. Its artists prefer to explore their own inner world, in contrast to the duty of painting to order. This chapter explores the way in which pictures themselves can be used to make a still-life grouping in a room, whether or not their subject matter is actually still life.

Above A delightful cluster of pictures and objects has been arranged with a still-life theme. Mantelpieces lend themselves well to these groupings in which small pictures usually work better than large ones.

Left A portrait adds personality to this shrine-like grouping on a shelf with a recessed panel. Objects can often assume an almost human quality in a setting like this.

Left In this rich world of pictures and things there is no obvious connection between the objects and images, but they create a lively conversation among themselves which gives them immediate visual appeal. The pictures are propped up rather than hung, implying that the elements could easily be rearranged.

COMPLEMENTARY ENSEMBLES

The domestic quality of most still-life art lends itself to an interaction with the room in which it is displayed. In addition, paintings that are not themselves still lifes may be used to form real-life groupings of objects, rather than being hung more formally on the wall. Casual placing of smaller-scale pictures, propped on a mantelpiece or hung somewhere near the floor, adds a valuable dimension to the richness and intimacy of a room. If the subject of the picture is itself a still life, then its relationship with a group of neighbouring objects can complement the picture, drawing the eye into the pictorial space.

The combination of pictures and sculpture is one of the delights of arranging a collection. Fewer people buy domestically scaled sculpture than buy pictures. However, the two forms of art usually complement each other extremely well because the sculpture helps to bring the picture into relief, even if there is no direct connection of subject or form. What is so satisfying about the mantelshelf ensemble on the right is that the additional sculptural objects are so much plainer than the typically Surrealist montage of horses and fragmented architecture next to them on the shelf, yet they are still in the same spirit of classical ruins and metaphysical geometry. The other examples on these pages show the various kinds of resemblances between pictures and objects drawn from the wide range of possibilities.

Paul Cézanne (1839–1906), one of the founders of modern art, spent the most important years of his life in provincial obscurity at Aix-en-Provence in the south of France (an obscurity many today

Above Cézanne's studio at Aix-en-Provence is an evocative place to visit. His paintings, such as this Renaissance cherub, are masterpieces of intense observation and can be seen in galleries all over the world.

Right Henri Gaudier-Brzeska's *The Dancer* (1913) demonstrates how small pieces of sculpture are a valuable counterpart to painting in a domestic setting. The three-dimensionality of the figure helps to give the painting depth.

would willingly share). Still life was one of his preoccupations. Few artists have done more to immortalize quite ordinary apples. His studio is preserved as a museum and includes a plastercast of a Renaissance cherub that he frequently drew and included in groupings of other objects. Of course, he did not arrange it to be viewed in the slightly self-conscious way that it is seen today, but it serves as a reminder of his pivotal achievement.

The sculpture of a dancer by Henri Gaudier-Brzeska (1891–1915), made just before the First World War, is in a setting that encourages you to move around it, partly because of the round table on which it stands. Bronze sculptures like these are expensive, but many artists make terracotta figures which are more affordable and have a timeless quality, evoking the art of the Etruscans and ancient Romans. Low relief, which has a flat back but a modelled surface, is less commonly found but also makes an effective bridge between the worlds of painting and sculpture. Plastercasts of sculptures and reliefs were popular in the nineteenth century and then went completely out of fashion. Some museums and galleries offer them for sale and, although they have a rather dead surface compared to original works, they can be used to make effective groupings with paintings.

All these examples show how a more or less subtle kind of double-take between a picture and its immediate context is capable of being an enriching experience, both on a purely formal plane and in terms of symbolism and meaning. Often, an accidental placing of things, done without much calculation, turns out to reveal its significance when you stand back to think about it in a more detached way.

Above The composition of this Surrealist picture in the style of Giorgio de Chirico with its *object-trouvé* decoration of scallop shell, classical bust and twirly rope creates an enigmatic miniature imaginative world.

FAMILIES OF OBJECTS

There is a special skill involved in bringing groups of objects together. It is helpful to think of them in families, because as in families they will come in different shapes and sizes, and will make you look closely for the resemblances and differences between them. The selection of such groups is better made by intuition than by logic. When you find that things just 'work' together, there is probably a good reason, even though it was not consciously thought through.

The examples illustrated on these pages show how diverse still-life families can be, involving a variety of pictures, framed and unframed, and a mixture of sculpture with natural and man-made objects. Such juxtaposed pieces can work in harmony to create unexpected and enjoyable dialogues.

Colour, form and texture may all be used to achieve this sense of natural relationships, but a sense of the absurd and incongruous is important as well. Part of the fun is to elevate things that have caught your eye, but which someone else might dismiss as junk, by putting them on a pedestal – though not necessarily a literal one – in the company of other, more obviously valuable things.

The subjects of still-life paintings themselves can offer ideas for families of objects, since they have been selected by an artist's eye and then transformed into art.

Above The smartly dressed boy might have sailed this antique pond yacht in bygone years. He looks prepared for adventure. The three figures, superficially similar but also very different from each other, are all the more effective because they partially mask the photograph.

A STRIKING MATCH

Many of the best visual objects are valueless in financial terms. They are frequently left to languish in a forgotten corner until someone casts a creative eye on them, and sees the way in which they can be used to advantage in a domestic still-life context.

Texture and colour play an important part in making groups of objects work around a picture. In still-life groups there is also the possibility of creating subtle, formal echoes, in which one object in the interior can begin to take on the attributes of an object or form in a nearby picture. 'The chance encounter of a sewing machine and an umbrella upon an operating table,' was the correct definition of poetry, according to the nineteenth-century French writer de Lautréamont, who thus inspired the Surrealist movement. In such unlikely couplings, the spark of metaphor can, like an old-fashioned match, be struck anywhere about the house, and illuminate a whole interior.

It is particularly gratifying when objects begin to work on several different levels at once. This sort of dialogue works best when there is some obvious basis of similarity, such as a single dominant colour, material or shape, as one might get in a large bowl full of wooden spoons and other implements. The objects brought together by these means have a common thread but in many ways are very different – some are rare and valuable, others not.

Far left This strongly symmetrical painting looks good propped on top of the cupboard, its receding perspective aided by its leaning back. The bowl of fruit in the foreground helps to continue the illusion of space.

Left This still-life ensemble is subtly constructed with 'rhymes' of colour, texture and form, such as the circular brass drawer-pull and the gold earring on the sculpted head. The shape of the head is echoed in the oval forms of the painting.

Previous page The identities of
the pictures of contrasting types
in this austere bedroom are
quietly reinforced by the objects
that stand beneath them.
The row of pots, for example,
complements the colours and
rhythmic character of the abstract
work above the cupboard.

Right It was an inspired idea to
place this wooden sculpture on
the floor between flights of
stairs, where it will look different
as the viewer moves around and
above it. The wall relief with its
bobbins also responds well to
a moving viewer with its depth
and shifting parallax.

Left A wire mesh shoe, presumably for arranging flowers in a bed of moss, could surely only have originated in France. It seems to have formed an alliance with the delicate period portrait drawing, in a charming ensemble of objects.

SPEAKING LOUDER THAN WORDS

The idea that art is a form of non-verbal language sounds quite reasonable, but because it does not have the same kind of precise meaning that verbal language has, we tend to doubt its ability to communicate. Living with pictures and taking an active role in placing them in a home is a kind of training in the language of art, and a way of discovering the things that shapes and colours can say. The association between objects and pictures in still-life groupings is one of the best ways of exercising such knowledge.

Rather sadly, perhaps, most museums do not mix their pictures with works of decorative art in their gallery displays, so therefore we get the impression that pictures ought to be seen against a neutral background. At home, however, it is a different matter. Rooms can seldom be set aside exclusively for pictures and we therefore need to develop a general sense of the affinity between pictures and other things. When grouping pictures and still-life objects, the scale can be large or small, and objects may be numerous or sparse, as the photographs on these pages indicate. Do not worry unduly about cluttering the space: a room can actually seem to get bigger the more things there are in it, provided that the scale is appropriate throughout and the objects well selected.

With pictures that evoke a definite historical period or a definite culture, there is a case for enlarging the meaning of the picture with associated objects from the same time or place. An alternative strategy is to balance the qualities of the picture with objects that introduce a degree of stimulating difference, or 'otherness' to use a word that often occurs in art criticism. This can often create a richer form of visual language. Instead of objects that are understood as ornaments, it can also look most effective to add to a still life things that have their origin in functional use, such as old vessels and tools. It is very much a matter of personal taste, however. The important thing is to enjoy as much as possible the pleasure of assembling and altering these arrangements as a form of communication through visual means.

ARTISTS' STUDIOS

The production of art is a finely tuned mixture of organization and randomness. Individual artists may veer in one direction or the other, but without an element of each, the art will fail through one-sidedness. Having a studio does not imply a cliché, such as the decorative chaos of a Parisian garret, although the reality of a cold room and lack of home comfort is perhaps part of the spur to getting on with it.

All creative working spaces are to some extent personalized and become a dependable aspect of the production of the work. Artists' studios are usually visually appealing, partly because they are semi-private and not arranged in a particularly formal or too self-conscious way. Materials and tools are stacked, ready and waiting. Old work is put out of sight to allow space for new. The objects, which are moved about the space, are in a condition of flux, always revealing something about the artist's personality and often offering inspired ideas for the home. Many artists' studios have been turned into museums, slightly melancholy in their suspended animation, but nonetheless valuable as an insight into the sources of creativity.

Right Art in action. The artist works on a large sheet of paper pinned to the wall in a comfortable-looking studio, with sunlight that certainly does not come from the north, the conventional direction of light for most purpose-built studios.

Left Canvases are stacked on top of a plan chest in a typical messy corner of an artist's studio. The abundance of work suggests that art is the by-product of a life of visual research and investigation, rather than a commodity produced in the hope of sale.

Below By contrast with the picture on the left, order reigns in the studio of artist David Gentleman, with sketchbook spreads for one of his popular travel volumes on the wall, above neatly organized brushes and pencils.

MINIMALISM

Minimalism has been a fashionable style of interior decoration for some years, offering a breath of fresh air in place of accumulated possessions. Those of us who are not quite capable of achieving its monastic levels of simplicity tend to suspect that owners of minimalist houses and apartments have cupboards overflowing with surplus objects somewhere out of sight. But the ideal, at least, of a simple life remains a potent one. Minimalism also has the benefit of encouraging architects and interior designers to use high-quality materials and finishes, as these are remorselessly exposed to view.

Although minimalism is associated with modernism, essentially it is timeless and has affinities with some of the earliest and most beautiful objects found in museums, which are frequently displayed in a minimalist manner. The quality of materials and images seems always to be amplified by the inherent simplicity of a minimalist setting.

In the home, minimalist rooms make attractive settings for pictures, offering little visual competition and often encouraging the soft fall of light onto plaster and wooden floorboards. The sense of visual focus that these settings create enhances the quality of all styles of pictures and frames although, as other sections of this book indicate, there are many ways of integrating pictures in rooms rich in colour and decorative detail.

Minimalism is also a style of art in its own right, dating from the 1950s. It has been through a number of transformations and even though it initially inspired contempt and disbelief from many art lovers, it continues to be a strong influence on contemporary painters and sculptors. Not surprisingly, minimalist art looks best in minimalist interiors.

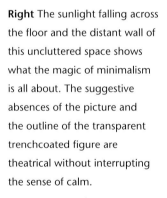

Right The sunlight falling across the floor and the distant wall of this uncluttered space shows what the magic of minimalism is all about. The suggestive absences of the picture and the outline of the transparent trenchcoated figure are theatrical without interrupting the sense of calm.

Above The way the pictures are hung, mostly straight onto the walls without frames, is designed to draw the eye deep into the room. It is important to be able to see the edges and corners of a minimalist room, even one arranged quite informally like this.

Left The art piece, typical of minimalist practice, has been carefully mounted for effect, with its vertical projections corresponding to the shelves seen beyond the window. The furniture and table all help to make a play with light across the simple wooden floor.

LESSONS ABOUT LESS

Minimalism in architecture and interior decoration is not so much a movement as a state of mind that recurs periodically throughout history. Its influence on contemporary interior decoration shows that its suggestion of austerity appeals strongly in a world crowded with objects. Current minimalist style is contemplative and inward-looking: the world outside the minimalist apartment or house is often a dense and over-crowded urban environment, and the designer aims to create an alternative inner landscape that inspires contemplation and serenity. Minimalist interiors can often look like monastic cells as designers aim at a return to authenticity of surfaces, without any coverings on either walls or floors. The minimalist designer also tries to present internal space in a simple way, as pure space. If you think that all interiors should be spacious, the minimalist designer is ready to heighten your perception, especially by modulating light within the room.

The minimalist effect is not generally as easy to achieve as it appears. The effectiveness of the look of the minimalist interior is loaded onto a few objects, and the sense of their relationship is crucial to a feeling of harmony. They demand a particularly fine tuning to give the effect of a string quartet, rather than a full orchestra.

Pictures usually look particularly good in minimalist settings, since there is so little else to distract the eye. However, the principles of space are paramount. Pictures need to be part of a spatial system in the room, which usually means that one wall is selected as the 'picture wall' and the others are left bare. This picture wall may not necessarily be the focus of the

Below The illusionistic picture shows another room, which seems ordinary until you notice the man lying on the floor, like a scene from a Hitchcock film. Just visible behind the fireplace is a mysterious top-lit extension of the space, a good example of minimalism's ability to alter ordinary perceptions of rooms.

Left The phrase 'Not very much of anything, but all truly elegant,' which children's writer Beatrix Potter used to describe the dinner party of her character Johnny Town Mouse, would equally apply to this cool but lively grouping, lit so brilliantly from above.

Below Like an eye-catching object in a landscape, this square red painting looks its best because of the carefully considered setting and the long distance from which it can be seen through a vista of all-white doors, leading you on into the brightly lit space beyond.

seating around a fire. It may be opposite the door, so that it is immediately visible on entry. In fact, this can be a better way to appreciate the pictures, as in ordinary daily life it is often better to view a picture obliquely, rather than facing it, which tends to diminish the quality of space. A good natural light from the side is desirable, so it is a good idea to avoid hanging a picture on the wall directly opposite the main windows.

The height of a picture in a room is crucial, particularly if only a single work is being hung. When sitting down, especially if the furniture is close to the ground, the natural eye-level is much lower than when the viewer is standing. It is important to decide which eye-level the pictures are being hung for, and to choose one consciously, rather than compromising somewhere between the two. It is difficult to make rules about this, because each case is different, but fortunately, it is easy to test different heights and discover what seems to work best. Conventionally, pictures are placed so that the midway height of the wall is about two-thirds of the way down the picture, creating an essentially classical relationship between the respective distances to floor and ceiling. This may prove to be the best height, but not necessarily. The most likely alternative will be a low eye-level, which will interact with the floor plane, an aspect of the room that is a key consideration in a minimalist design.

Right A room with a beautiful quality of light, coming from various kinds of window. The stove in the foreground, with its pair of solid shapes, forms a necessary foreground to the group of daybed, standard light and scroll in the distance.

SIMPLE YET COMPLEX

The creation of an effective minimalist space involves more than just the absence of decoration. As well as high-quality finishes, there needs to be some element of complexity to ensure that the room becomes something other than just the inside of a plain box. A designer starting from scratch on a new project, even if it is a conversion in an existing shell, may have no difficulty in forming the space to create a sense of sequence and direction. However, other projects may not offer the luxury of a premeditated minimalist design, and different means will have to be found to articulate the space. The placing of a picture within the scheme may therefore add a crucial element of focus, acting like the end point of a walk.

As in a well-designed landscape, it is a good idea to extend the sense of a journey with a little optical illusion, particularly if the space available is not very extensive – the mind seems to enjoy such diversions. In interior design terms, this could imply making a foreground, with objects such as bowls or stones at a low level, ensuring a kind of starting line for the journey. It is also helpful to provide something in the middle distance as a resting point, which can be more difficult to get right. A piece of furniture might work, or a feature such as a spur wall, projecting like the side wings of a traditional theatre. A well-placed bookcase can act as a form of room-divider, perhaps presenting a blank back to the main direction of the approach. This can also have the advantage of masking direct light from a window beyond, so that the light is thrown onto the picture without the glare from the window. The space beyond would make a pleasingly intimate corner for reading.

The heightened awareness of objects that minimalism encourages means that various simple games become tremendously satisfying. Rhythms and echoes of simple numbers enable the eye to set up links between pictures and furniture or other aspects of the room.

Below A room in a converted building that offers a variety of spatial experiences. The grouping of three pictures, spotlights and cushions at the far end helps to give a classical structure. Note how the base of the walls is recessed with a 'flash gap' detail to give a floating effect.

Above A seemingly casual grouping of pictures and furniture has enough structure in its unity of colour and repetition of paired objects to look almost formal. Here is a room that could be lived in, unlike some more 'perfect' minimalist interiors.

Previous page An old master painting displayed as a free-standing screen: a novel idea from Philip Johnson's famous Glass House, Connecticut of 1949.

Connections can form almost unconsciously when things fall into place as a result of a particular lifestyle or sense of order, but the conscious placing of pictures can bring them into view and articulate the kind of non-verbal associations that link things almost like a private joke.

An acquaintance with contemporary art and its ways of filling space, as well as walls, can be useful. Much art today consists of installations that create a heightened awareness of the presence of objects in space. You can use this to preserve or recapture that quality of space that is often at its most attractive when you first move into a new home, before too many things take possession and the intrinsic character of the space begins to recede.

As well as illustrating the above points, the rooms on these pages play with the simple idea of 'two-ness', in which objects may be paired like identical or non-identical twins. Two is a much less stable number than three in the visual world, because it is always threatening to split into separate parts, and the cultivation of visual dualities depends on the implication, at least, of an overall unifying form, or on some kind of difference between the twinned objects that overcomes the illusion of seeing double. When this balance is struck, the result is dynamic and lively.

Left A witty grouping of paired sinks and pictures that heightens perception and allows asymmetrical objects to look almost as if they were 'on stage'.

Below A contemplative picture, which extends the space in the small bedroom and brings a restful horizontal line parallel with the bed itself. The switch-plate in the foreground sets up a formal relationship with the rectangle of the picture beyond and becomes an object of interest in its own right.

ART GALLERIES

Recently established art galleries, especially the smaller ones, are a valuable source of inspiration for designing minimalist-style rooms based around pictures. Many dealers now commission good architects to build or convert their spaces, and they bring their own experience of hanging pictures to the commission. Some element of top lighting, such as skylights, is a luxury that city art dealers can seldom afford, but in two of the examples shown here, both in rural settings, different sources of light are used to provide a good level of illumination without dazzle; the light is reflected and filtered before it reaches the pictures. This type of lighting is also better for conservation purposes than direct lighting. Skylights and other effects like these can be built in domestic settings where there is no building above, and greatly improve the illumination by bringing light into the inner side of the room. The quality of the light will vary according to the direction the skylight faces.

Art galleries demonstrate how in an empty space the eye is drawn to the floor and especially to the junction between the floor and the walls. The aversion of minimalist architects to skirting boards at times seems impractical, but it is vital to articulating the space cleanly. Often a recessed channel, made of extruded metal, is used to provide an edge against which the plasterer can work.

Left The interior of the Art Sway Gallery near Lymington, England, by architect Tony Fretton is far from a blank, neutral space. In its austere discipline it concentrates viewers' attention on the pictures, while still retaining a personality of its own.

Left The gallery at Roche Court, Wiltshire, for the New Art Centre by Munkenbeck and Marshall, shows the value of different floor levels and a concealed light source. The full-height windows look out onto open landscape.

Left A suggestive space that could hardly be simpler, but which is a good setting for art that requires concentrated, meditative viewing.

GROUPINGS AND SEQUENCES

If minimalism establishes the ground rules for deploying a small number of pictures, then other forms of order must be found to cope with the probability that people who love pictures will have many of them.

There are several different kinds of picture groups. Works by the same artist, or in a similar style, constitute an obvious category. Works of similar colour or medium, such as prints, look attractive in a close-knit grouping. Prints have often been issued in sets, for example William Hogarth's *The Rake's Progress* (1735), which tells the story in eight scenes of the downfall of a thoughtless young man in Georgian London. Even prints that do not need to be seen as a complete set, like a series of views by the same artist, are satisfying to look at as a group and make an impact by their uniformity.

In historic collections, one can often find a group of pictures united by having the same kind of frame or even by being approximately the same size. In the days when portrait painting was a trade, rather as portrait photography usually is today, instead of high art, there were standard-size canvases that fitted standard frames, so that framers could make the frames for stock and then painters could swop canvases from one frame to another. In this way, it was possible to assemble your ancestors in rows, all painted to a similar scale.

Left Pin-up pictures are grouped in frames of differing sizes, but organized in three rows on the wall. The different poses work almost like a sequence of film frames.

Right Black-and-white engravings have been given an original context in this conjunction with a collection of hand mirrors and other tools of the hairdresser's craft. The abstract pattern that results is delightful and unexpected.

ROWS OF IMAGES

The multiplication of similar images, identically framed, creates a strong decorative effect, which is often more than the sum of its individual parts, giving a rhythm and order to the wall. These pictures can be arranged in a pattern like a checkerboard, with everything in rows and columns, or can be staggered in the same way as a brick wall. Alternatively, the rhythm may be syncopated by adding larger and smaller intervals of space between the lines of the pictures.

Many sets of prints that hang as groups were originally published in book form, but dealers have little compunction about splitting up illustrated books with attractive plates, since the parts are worth more than the whole. Conscience must decide whether a dismembered book gives more pleasure in this form than it would if kept on a shelf and only occasionally looked at. Sensibly, some contemporary illustrated special editions are issued with loose sets of prints so that you can decide to have them on the wall without damaging the book.

A series hung in this way has a unique fascination and, assuming the images have a visual consistency, the strong pattern will encourage people to take a closer look. For this purpose, it is best if no other pictures are allowed in the vicinity to disturb the unity of effect.

Left Cartoons of nineteenth-century public figures are still compatible with a modern room, hung in carefully composed rows with matching frames. Against this impressive order, a few crooked frames contribute some liveliness, while the wall as a whole helps to reflect light from the window.

Left Individual photographic portraits in box frames projecting forwards add a pleasing pattern of shadow to the wall, bringing it to three-dimensional life and enhancing the interest of the images themselves.

PICTURE COLLECTIONS

The groupings of pictures often reveal the interests of a serious collector. While some art lovers prefer to browse and pick pictures by taste and association, forming eclectic ensembles of favourite pieces, others prefer to make their home almost into a miniature museum, in which you expect to find linkages between the works on show. While this may sound rather dry and academic, it is one of the pleasures of collecting that can be passed on to visitors and friends. A collector is like someone gathering fragments from the shipwreck of time and meticulously putting them back into order.

Where a series of original art works is concerned, it is a rare but inspired action to purchase the whole lot and enjoy the unity of the resulting ensemble. To make this bold decision is to perform a service to the artist, especially if he or she is still living. In addition, the collector may justifiably be proud of having not only one unique original, but something that amplifies the effect of uniqueness by extending its identity into a sequence that mirrors the artist's original intentions.

Below Posters from the period between the two world wars like these were often the work of celebrated artists. They look good grouped together, with their eye-catching relationship between text and image, rendered in the soft lithographic printing of the time.

Right Not posters, but an enigmatic and disturbing collection of words and images placed in deadpan manner, without frames, at the head of a staircase where they have a strong impact. This encourages the formation of new associations among images when passing by, since moving past art, rather than just sitting and staring at it, often leads to fresh ideas and interpretations.

PLEASING SEQUENCES

Hanging groups of pictures successfully depends a lot on a sense of rhythm. It is relatively easy to hang a group of similar works, but dealing with pictures that display contrasts of scale, colour and medium is more difficult, and by the same token, more rewarding when it comes out right.

First it is necessary to identify pairs or groups of three that seem to go together. In the Western world, at least, our eyes are trained to move from left to right because that is the direction in which we write. It is important, therefore, to imagine this as the instinctive way of scanning a group of pictures, and then consider the sequence almost in musical terms as a single phrase, that must begin, continue, and come to an end. Nothing should stand out too strongly, but neither should there be too much sameness.

Avoid scattered and overpacked effects, neither of which have any structure. However, the best results come not from any formula involving correct numbers or optimum density, but from the coherence and visual logic of the arrangement. Not only the sequence, but the relative spaces between the pictures are important, as are their relative heights.

When grouping small pictures it is important to consider the features of the room and the placing of the furniture, as well as the intrinsic character of the works themselves. Looking at certain abstract paintings that organize rectangular shapes on a flat surface could be a useful

Right An apparently casual arrangement of pictures reveals an underlying rhythmic structure, moving from bottom left to top right in an ascending diagonal, and then falling to the picture over the fireplace.

guide for this kind of hanging, but so could observations from everyday life. The geometry of a shop front, with a pattern of shapes and colours in the window could provide a moment of inspiration, as could an arrangement of parked cars seen from a high window. Looking for accidental patterns in the everyday world is a special pleasure and costs absolutely nothing.

Grouping effects tend to become easier to achieve when there is a more crowded 'hang' of items on the wall, but it is a matter of personal temperament whether you like things cluttered or not. The example shown above is more subtle than it looks, because it blends old prints of English monarchs with modern photographs, making an implied connection between the two, and then varies the menu with a selection of other old prints, related in colour to the monarchs but very different in subject. The result is the opposite of stuffy formality. It has a pleasingly casual air of being thrown together with the characteristic that Stendhal liked to attribute to the English of 'le carefully careless'.

Above A jolly jumble of old prints on a pin-up board attains unity through its underlying grid structure and enclosing frame. The family photographs on the shelf below, joining the medieval monarchs and croquet-playing bears, look more at ease than they would in conventional frames.

CHOOSING BACKGROUNDS

Relationships of scale and colour have already been mentioned as one of the key factors in making picture groupings. The examples shown on these pages have shared characteristics such as photographs, but this on its own would not ensure that they make good groupings. The secret of success in these instances seems to come from their variety of frame size, combined with a common base line, provided by floor or shelf, which helps to draw attention to the variation in frame size, seen against a broad background. It is a simple pleasure, perhaps, to sit and contemplate rectangles and their proportions, but many architects like to spend their time in such reverie. Where several rectangles come into the same field of view, the eye may perform an elaborate involuntary dance between them.

The best way to set up such simple but satisfying relationships is probably to let yourself be guided by intuition. Try putting down the intended group of pictures in a possible position without much forethought, and see whether the effect seems right. You may well have a lucky break and this random scattering will work well; if not, the occasional casual tweak when passing will probably achieve a better result than serious analysis.

Below Polaroid prints, unlike conventional photos, have the advantage of being strong enough to lean against a wall without curling up or being blown away. Their white borders help to unify this casual but disciplined kitchen grouping.

Left With a view like this, who needs pictures? The framed photographs nonetheless provide a close-up focus of interest amidst other assorted black-and-white objects, and would become far more prominent at night.

PICTURES AND THEIR ASSOCIATIONS

The positioning of a sequence of pictures in relation to the objects immediately surrounding it can build up additional layers of meaning. Here, the rich non-verbal language of signs and symbols comes into play, and witty juxtapositions operate like jokes in which objects may be connected by a string of inverted logic, as well as by more direct association. Connections, such as a recurrent use of line or of a certain colour, can help to link the formal aspects of the works, as well as set up echoes between the similar forms of dissimilar objects, giving them a sort of metaphorically shared identity. In the grouping below, for example, there is a sophisticated visual synthesis at work: the spider, for example, seems to link via the glass disk below, with its juxtaposition of fish and knife, to the spoked wheels of the trolley that is acting as a side-table.

The composite image on the right is a single work by the British artists Gilbert & George that is designed to be displayed in a very specific manner. While an imposing work in its own right, it is also complemented by the careful choice of furniture, making a harsh, striking world of black, white and metallic surfaces, which the red roses hardly mitigate.

Left Wisdom, wit and weirdness are allied in this grouping. There is no need for the frames to match, since randomness is the principle underlying the assembly. As with most unorganized sequences, however, unexpected patterns and similarities begin to emerge.

Right This artwork by Gilbert & George is designed to be hung in a very precise configuration, since it plays on the reflections in the room. It lends a special quality of depth to this closed corner with its formal arrangement of two chairs and a table.

This internal staircase to nowhere, built to provide headroom for a descending stair below, has resulted in a characterful conjunction of books and pictures. The irregular outline of the descending steps allows small pictures to occupy their own niches in a hanging pattern intended to avoid regularity of grouping and allow for a variety of styles and subjects.

PERSONAL SPACES

The larger the number of images on a wall, the greater the opportunities the mind has for playing games of association between colour, shape and theme. The frames of pictures also have a part to play in developing subliminal links in which the subconscious mind uses the logic of dreams to superimpose one image on another, leaving the waking mind struggling to catch up and bring in a conscious understanding of meaning.

Perhaps a bedroom is a particularly suitable place to play this kind of game. Some writers imply that even the pictures we have long since ceased to take in as a conscious part of our surroundings are likely to influence some area of the mind from which dreams also emerge, with their baffling but often meaningful insights into our lives and the lives of others.

On a simpler level, the choices about what pictures to hang in our more intimate surroundings are likely to reveal something about our personalities – even things we do not quite understand ourselves.

Above Drawings simply framed in a corner of the bedroom are hung to give the impression of stairs going downwards out of sight. The wall-mounted radiator might have looked obtrusive, but the pictures help to integrate it into the decorative scheme.

Left The small-scale details of the pictures in this bedroom, many of them with a vegetation theme or images of the moon, are a source of endless fascination. The witty improvised bedside lamp picks up the theme of botanical illustration from the picture hanging above it.

Opposite If you feel lonely in this bed, you can choose from a wide variety of companions assembled on the wall behind you. The gilded frames of some of these photographs give a twist to the group and match the carved bedposts.

Order and chaos are the twin poles between which most households revolve. Each has its own particular pleasures. As contemporary science tells us, chaos is another form of order that merely requires a different way of looking. Any successful underlying structure will allow the tides of life to ebb and flow around it.

Once they have been hung, pictures are elements of a room that are usually left in position, even when other things change around them. They can therefore establish a structure of order, and create the quality of calm that most people look to their physical surroundings to provide.

Formality in hanging can be completely appropriate, depending on the pictures themselves and the mood that is wanted for the room as a whole. A forced informality without any basis in logic or in the content of the pictures themselves can, by contrast, be intensely irritating, so it may be better to follow the natural instinct towards regularity and symmetry. It's a question of personal choice and temperament that is likely to come through in the style of the whole house.

The architectural and decorative prints on these pages are standardized in colour and visual impact, so that they suggest a regular hanging pattern. The group on the right is well adjusted to the formality of the twin chairs and candle brackets, centred on a pedestal pier table, but the informal 'tablescape' and the comfortable chair in the foreground provide a sufficient degree of contrast.

Left Framed architectural prints are attractive and very popular. On this austere staircase, prints of buildings on one landing link, appropriately enough, with a group of four Roman emperors on another.

Right These intricate designs demand a symmetrical layout, which accords well with their own internal organization. The colour scheme of the room with its restrained warm greys helps to emphasize the prints.

OFF THE WALL

Walls seem to be the natural place for pictures, but when on the wall they can seem remote. Once in position, pictures are only ever seen in certain light conditions. A picture more casually displayed by leaning it against a wall or by ranging it on a shelf, can be picked up easily, moved into different lights and held in the hands.

This might imply a degree of disrespect, but pictures need to be brought into a close and stimulating relationship with life rather than placed at a distance. This physical relationship with pictures as objects is one of the pleasures of ownership. It is possible to get quite excited about the backs of pictures, which may carry some vital evidence of identification, or even a set of old labels indicating where a particular picture was framed, displayed and sold. It is also nice to be able to hand a picture to someone else to hold and admire, as one might with a baby.

Above The fireplace is probably never used, but the casually placed picture makes an unusual and eye-catching feature.

Left Framed drawings standing three-deep on a shelf are far more likely to invite handling than if they were simply hung on a wall. Books and small pictures always look good together on shelves.

Right This picture gains in effect from standing on an easel, which introduces diagonal lines into a composition of horizontals and verticals. Pictures painted on concrete or other heavy materials, as well as carved stone inscriptions, are often best carried on easels in this manner, especially if the walls are not strong enough to hold them.

MOODS

Living in harmony with one's surroundings could imply a degree of monotony, in which nothing speaks too loudly to disturb the overall calm. Certainly it would seem that this is appealing to many people, since shops and department stores are full of agreeably bland furnishings that combine together like a set of ice-cream flavours, avoiding any danger of getting it wrong. They may be consumed at ice-cream speed, too, rather than imposing any longer-term commitment.

A more individual approach to decorating a room demands a certain amount of risk, but involves some enjoyable elements of discovery. It is important to have a degree of conviction, to feel able to back your own instinctive judgment about the quality of material things. Setting up home for the first time, even in a student hostel or a small rented flat, is a moment of definition and liberation. Even an office workspace can be personalized by a postcard of a painting from a museum pinned up, acting as a kind of visiting card that tells others what kind of person you are. Some of these images may acquire a talismanic quality, being taken from place to place in the course of life.

Right The holiday informality of this room makes a V-shaped string from a picture hook an appropriate method of hanging. The rhythm of the pictures, matching the space between the shelf brackets, gives coherence.

Changing contexts will alter their meaning and keep them fresh. A picture or print, once acquired, may be worth keeping, since it can be welcomed back later as a period piece or a memory of times past. Some instinctive choices turn out to have more significance than was realized at the time.

When choosing images to create a mood, there is no need to distinguish between fine art and the variety of other imagery that can fill a house. This awareness has, almost unknowingly, been one of the great liberations of the last thirty years or so. Time was when the externals of fine art, such as gilt frames, were perceived as part of its status, and were used to justify hanging indifferent or even downright dreadful works in pursuit of some notion of what art ought to be. However, in the age of mass visual reproduction, anything goes. Ever since the Cubists started pasting pieces of newspaper into their collages, it has often been the unconventional eyes of artists themselves that have led others to appreciate the quality of discarded or neglected imagery.

Above These luscious enlarged apricots bring softness and warmth to the metallic objects in the foreground. Furnishing dining rooms with pictures of food dates back to the eighteenth century.

Right An informal childlike artwork with irregular edges animates the space of this recess. Although the formal elements of the room are rather rigid, the objects bring it to life.

THE RIGHT LIGHT

The quality of natural light seems to be one of the unalterable aspects of a house or apartment, since it depends on window size, surroundings and orientation. When looking at a home as a prospective buyer or tenant, one seldom gets the chance to experience the whole range of light qualities that occur in each room throughout the day, let alone throughout the seasons of the year, but the art of tuning an interior to bring out its individual character depends on understanding the varied potential that will exist in all interiors. Low light in the morning and evening, for example, is always especially beautiful.

Pictures may seem less directly involved in the manipulation of light compared with curtains, blinds, wall colours and surfaces, but there is an art in selecting pictures that help to create a mood in a particular place, in relation to the light. Pictures benefit from an association between their colour and tone and that of their background. A dark picture may look good in a dark corner of a room, emphasizing what already exists. If it hangs in too much light, the result could be an excessive amount of reflection from the glass, or from the varnish if it is an unframed oil painting. Light pictures, on the other hand, need lighter surroundings. The white walls so commonly found in galleries have the virtue of neutrality, but are not always the most flattering background to art as they also tend to generate a cold quality of light.

Left Light falls beautifully onto the rough plaster walls of this medieval house. The mellow tones of the woodwork are matched by the paintings, old and new.

Below Sunlight is lovely in this room in Eltham Palace, Greenwich, but not good for the resident watercolours by J.M.W. Turner. To prevent the room having to be kept dark for their sake, the owner Sir Stephen Courtauld had sliding wooden shutters fitted.

EXOTIC MOODS

Some rooms establish specific moods of place and time through associations of pictures and furnishings. Connoisseurs of the early Romantic period were among the first to indulge in this craving for the exotic experience, and it has proved an incentive to collectors ever since, as well as a means of surrounding works of art with a three-dimensional interpretation – an understanding of mood that really enhances the pleasure of ownership.

It is possible to go all the way in recreating a period room and collecting all the items needed can become an engrossing obsession. Such an effect however may look rather precious and detached from ordinary life. It is also an expensive hobby and is dependent on having a suitably proportioned empty shell to begin with. Something less extreme will achieve as good an effect and demonstrate a greater sense of flexibility and adaptation. Links and associations need to be made between pictures and other objects in the room, which, if they have the same cultural origin, are likely to share elements of visual language, such as pattern and colour.

If you create a room with an Eastern feel like those achieved in the interiors illustrated here, you should bear in mind that the level of seating affects the level at which you hang pictures. Western cultures have a relatively high sitting position that exerts a strong influence on the spatial feeling of the room and also on the eye-level at which works of art are usually viewed.

Left A collection of nineteenth-century oriental pictures, showing the Western world's romantic vision of the East, complements the luxurious L-shaped divan. The uplighters on the two main pictures help to create the intimate mood.

Below The interior of a Japanese house is evoked by the design of this room, while the lighting helps to highlight the variety of surfaces in the paintings, reproducing some of the liveliness of natural light. Everything is brought together in the warm tones of the pictures and woodwork.

LIGHT AND SPACE

It is easy enough to understand that rooms are made up of space, since we can measure it and know whether it is empty or full. More difficult to take in is the concept that space itself is composed of light, since this appears to be more subjective. Yet light modifies our perception of space and its changing quality makes a house into a kind of sundial. We forget too easily that it is our solid-seeming surroundings that are moving, not the apparently moving sun. In terms of physics, in any case, solid matter is only a particular configuration of the same kind of energy that creates light.

Such speculations may seem remote from everyday experience, but many contemporary architects are shifting their concern from space as a separate phenomenon towards a more conscious manipulation of light, often using different kinds of glass to diffuse available light within a room or to bring it into the darker parts of an interior. Quality of light in a room depends not only on the atmospheric conditions and the angle of the sun, but also on the type of window glass through which the light travels, and on the surface from which it is reflected into our eyes. As the interiors shown on these pages demonstrate, pictures are not incidental to this game, for their placing can help to enhance significantly the beauty of light, and can also modify the quality of space.

Previous page In the exquisite neatness of this modern room, the paintings strike an agreeable note of improvisation, hung as though in an auction house, some with, some without frames, and others leaning against the wall.

Left This hallway develops a complex mixture of associations with its varied objects. The commanding gaze of the portrait head adds to the strangeness created by the glazed partition that reflects light in the hallway as well as revealing glowing light within.

Right This simple but beautiful vaulted staircase will reflect the times of day as shifting daylight changes its mood. The picture hanging on the half-landing has an appropriate sense of turning and movement.

Above An object reflected in water or some irregular shiny surface must have produced the rippling shadow on the wall, which is echoed in the pattern of the larger black-and-white photograph on the cupboard.

PHOTOGRAPHIC SOLUTIONS

Photographs are increasingly valued as objects in interior decoration. 'Knowledge of photography is just as important as that of the alphabet,' said László Moholy-Nagy, a teacher at the famous Bauhaus in Germany in the 1920s, 'the illiterates of the future will be ignorant of the use of camera and pen alike.' Photography and video have indeed come to play an increasing part in the creation of all kinds of art. Despite the universal availability of colour, back and white remains the preferred medium for most serious art photographers, and is often preferred for everyday imagery too because of the greater degree of unity and abstraction in the images it presents. Black-and-white photographs certainly look authoritative and stylish when hung as posters or framed pictures in the home.

Photographs usually look better if they are in some way differentiated from other works of art, either in their framing or their mode of display. It is possible to display many different sorts of photographs effectively, from valuable original prints by famous artists to family snaps. Most, however, usually look best in simple frames. They can be window-mounted or 'float-mounted', so that the edge of the paper is visible.

Sometimes the smoothness of photographic paper makes the image seem less alive than it should be. There are a number of hanging strategies to overcome this, including having appropriate textures in the vicinity of the photograph, for example a wall or a shelf surface with groups of objects. When photographs do not have a high collectable value, they can be displayed quite informally, as seen in some of the examples here; this helps to jump them into three dimensions, as objects that can be handled.

Left If babies crawl on the floor, why shouldn't their photographs? This is a perfect way of adding a touch of informality to a family portrait that might seem a little mannered hung on the wall.

Left Art rather than snapshot: the grey frames of this group of three photographs help to bring out the mid-tones of the images as well as the texture of the painted brick wall behind.

Right The 'distressed' surface of the frame of the picture in front is an appropriate way to draw attention to the beauty of texture in the old woman's face and arms. Its mid tone is better for this purpose than a strong black frame.

Left Simple but charming: family photos mounted on individual stands become personalities through this presentation, which also conveniently tilts the image upwards for easier viewing.

FRAMING YOUR IMAGE

Frames play an important role in the way pictures are presented and the impact they make. Like everything else that we have around us, they are a way of making a statement. Framing a picture well is largely a matter of context: judging the mood of a room and the picture correctly, and trying to make sure that they can live together.

In the past, frames were often an integral part of the picture, not only complementing it visually but carrying important symbolic meaning. Frames soon became relatively standardized, though their craftsmanship in carving and gilding remained as admirable in its way as the execution of the painting itself. The late nineteenth century in particular was a time of remarkable experimentation with frames. Some artists revived aspects of Renaissance practice, with elaborately gilded wood and *gesso*, while others, as van Gogh did on several occasions, extended the painting itself onto the surface of the frame.

The movement in the early twentieth century was in favour of the decontextualized work of art, stressing its universal validity rather than its quality of belonging to a particular place and time. There was consequently a reaction against making the picture part of the furnishings of a room through attending too much to the frame.

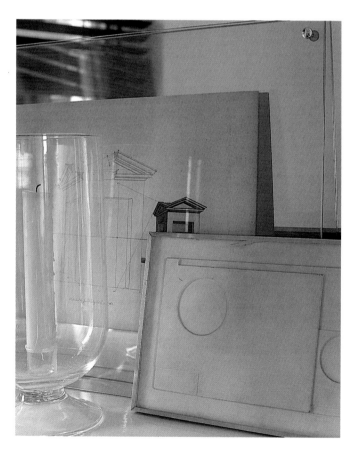

Left Geometry and space: a simple frame in the foreground on an abstract white relief is contrasted with an academic perspective diagram held between two sheets of acetate.

Right The rich frame on this tiny icon emphasizes its importance as an object of worship, and gives it the strength it needs to compete with the beautiful but overpowering hand-painted wallpaper.

EMBELLISHING FRAMES

Frames can offer more innocent fun than a visit to an average framer's shop might suggest. For example, if they are improvised out of pieces of joinery that were never intended for this purpose they help to draw attention to themselves by their ugly duckling quality.

A frame can be embellished in a number of ways, with ornaments made from objects such as shells or pine cones, or with various kinds of decorative paint finishes. The vogue for graining, combing and stippling walls and woodwork has declined from its height in the 1980s, but folk art examples of these techniques can still act as a stimulus. Such techniques are enjoyable to experiment with and the frame may become as much a work of art as the picture inside it – always make sure that your image can survive this strong competition! There are also folk art traditions well worth reviving that involve painting part of the mount on the back of the glass, using black with touches of gold.

It is important, of course, to retain a sense of appropriateness in relation to the work of art inside the frame, as well as to the mood of the room. Frames with decorative paint finishes are like strong flavours in food and need to strike the right note.

Above A window does service as a frame in this grouping by a staircase. Having its window ironmongery still attached helps to emphasize its deliberate incongruity.

Opposite The flat, heavy frames around these old maps would look too institutional in some rooms, but, hanging from picture rails in this plain setting, with its attractive timber boarding on walls, floor and ceiling, they have just the right workmanlike character.

Left The frame of this folk art inlay picture, depicting the railway bridge and castle at Conway, North Wales, is a fine example of decorative imitation graining made with a comb. This kind of finish is not difficult to reproduce with the right materials.

HISTORICAL FRAMES

A variety of historical frames hanging in one room helps to make the frames a focus of attention, without necessarily distracting from the pictures themselves. It is a good idea to look out for interesting frames when you are considering buying a picture. Sadly, there are many techniques which were practised in the past that have fallen out of use because the relevant skills have been lost through lack of demand. The technique for hanging is much the same as it is for any kind of picture grouping, but elements of consistency, contrast and balance in the frames become more of a conscious consideration.

A strong dark background colour, as seen in the rooms illustrated on these pages, usually sets off a group of historical frames well, bringing them into relief. Green and gold is a well-tried decorative combination that helps create a luxurious masculine feeling in an interior. Red is a traditional colour for use in picture galleries, and is usually associated with gold as the height of regal splendour. Both green and red can team well with black, which is probably the second favourite colour for picture frames after gold.

There are several varieties of gold leaf, which produce different effects of colour. As a hobby, gilding with real gold leaf requires some skill and training, but not much in the way of equipment. If you like the effect, it would be worth learning how to achieve it.

Right An eccentric corner, showing how frames can be used as a focus of attention in their own right, even when they have no pictures in them. The string of fairy lights is an unusual but not impractical way of lighting a picture.

Left Gilt frames are shown off to advantage in this rich and intimate room with dark-green walls, lovingly furnished in the style of the early nineteenth century. Pictures in the foreground are hung on a leaf of a folding screen.

These unusual photograph frames make a good match with the pressed metal icon frames for the devotional images behind. This is a group of objects that makes you wonder what it would be like to run your fingers over the different surfaces.

109

Left Posters and prints on giant large metallic panels, their scale enhanced by the small easel and frame on the floor below – a perfect way to retain the posters' contemporary feel.

Right Two enigmatic oriental heads look down from a stripped Baroque frame, adding mystery to an unexpected assembly of objects. A frame is a valuable way of focusing attention, even if it does not contain a conventional picture.

VISUAL JOKES

A frame is a means of protecting a picture from damage, but it is also a visual device, adding a kind of punch-line to the picture. The frame can reassert what the picture is saying, or it can subvert it to a greater or lesser extent in a form of straight-man/funny-man dialogue. As with the great comedy duos like Laurel and Hardy, each partner would be lost without the other, however much their act depends on an illusion of disagreement.

There is scope in framing for the mildly outrageous comment, delivered with a straight face. This may range from the subtle dislocation of scale caused by the tiny easel placed on the floor in the picture above, combined with the original way of presenting posters against two large panels, to the unexpected but convincing use in the room on the right of an empty frame containing two oriental stone heads in the midst of what appear to be surroundings of deep gravity. The inflatable frames in pastel colours in the picture alongside represent the kind of novelty that is best caught fresh, but here they belong effectively to the visual theme of the room and do not detract from the drawings framed inside them.

Calculated incongruity is one of the most effective ways of achieving a sense of individual style. There must be many more ways of framing and displaying pictures than have ever been tried out. Framing tends to be a conservative business, so that it is refreshing when new ideas come along. People can become over concerned with propriety in picture framing, but the individual eye must, as always, judge whether a deviation from the norm is a stroke of inspiration or a moment of folly. Sometimes you simply cannot know until you have tried it.

Below Inflatable frames like children's swimming aids suit the party spirit of this corner. Not all art would survive this treatment, but these drawings of heads are obviously in no way upset by their surroundings.

HISTORICAL STYLES

For art-lovers cultivating an eye for frames, there is much to enjoy. Carved and gilded frames have been in production continuously since the sixteenth century in a variety of styles, but the most attractive are probably those in the Baroque and Rococo styles of the seventeenth and eighteenth centuries. These offered most scope to the craftsman in terms of freedom of invention and exercise of technical skill. They have been imitated ever since, but it is worth seeking out original frames in great houses and museums to appreciate the sharpness of detail and overall sense of movement in the design.

The neo-classical style of the French Revolutionary period persisted for many years into the nineteenth century. It inspired the simple frames of progressive Victorian artists such as the Pre-Raphaelites and helped their intense paintings to glow in an aura of gold.

It is also worth studying the different kind of frames that were used for oil paintings, watercolours and prints. The smaller, domestically scaled frames of the nineteenth century often had a folk art quality of invention about them that modern frames can only recapture with difficulty. Colour lithographs based on anecdotal salon pictures, which ornamented country cottages, were displayed in simple birds-eye maple-veneered frames that were bolection-moulded and lined with a gold slip.

Above This beautiful carved frame in the Rococo style rewards hours of study, and looks better surrounding a mirror than a picture. The postcard of a famous image by Jacopo Pontormo (1494–1556), tucked in at the side, is a good throwaway touch.

Left A distinctive frame from the 1870s made for a Pre-Raphaelite painting. Artists liked the flat patterns of Regency reeding combined with disc ornaments taken from Japanese pottery.

Below The decorative bamboo frames with a slip of duck-egg blue that surround these fencing prints are an object of attention in their own right, adding to the period feel of the room without overpowering it.

Right The heavy gilded frames of the Baroque style belong with an integrated style of room, seen here with its matching wall coverings, furniture and carved marble chimneypiece, all bursting with energy.

Coming alive to the visual world through the medium of art is an exhilarating experience which turns convention on its head. A fresh eye transforms the everyday into the unexpected, sometimes even the miraculous. Amid much confusion and destruction, the styles of twentieth-century art broke all the barriers, leaving open a wide field of possibilities for those inspired enough to take them. There is no longer a single accepted way of doing things, and this applies to the creation of the home as a work of art as much as to creation of works of art themselves.

The breaking of barriers does not mean that all new effects will necessarily be successful nor that old ways of doing things will always look stale and meaningless. Decoration in the twentieth century went through several cycles of revolution and conservative backlash, neither of which seemed to produce enduringly satisfying answers. How could they? Decoration, whether amateur or professional, is a highly personal matter, not only in the sense that different people are culturally conditioned to like different things, but also because each person is a complex bundle of conflicting impulses.

Below Dappled deception, achieved with a photo mural of autumn foliage, against which the painted head appears to hang in space.

Right The centre of a large window is probably the last place most people would think of hanging a painting, but with a window of this size, it helps to focus the room and break up the excessive area of glass. If curtains were used here, it might be difficult to pass them behind the picture, but it would then achieve a double success in adding interest to what might otherwise be an overwhelming extent of fabric.

Above Picture, frame and backing have decided to live independent lives, helping to add to the dreamlike effect in this corridor.

CREATING THE UNEXPECTED

Some people steer sharply towards order, others towards disorder, but these are deceptive categories in themselves. Neither offers an automatic guarantee of finding the elusive goal of an interior that matches one's inner condition yet retains unexpected quirks – like a trusted but slightly unpredictable friend.

The element of surprise can arise from a number of factors. Of course, it may be inherent in the design of the home and a major asset to establishing character. However, let us suppose that this is not the case, and that a room's atmosphere must be created from the choice and disposition of objects. Pictures are only one of several types of things that contribute to the effect, but they have distinct advantages – their strong symbolism and the fact they are portable. It is well worth hanging pictures in a variety of different combinations and situations to discover what they look like. As a lonely child of rich parents, the art historian Kenneth Clark used to do this, practising for his future role as Director of the National Gallery in London as he periodically got the servants to rehang all the pictures under his supervision.

A home can be treated like a garden, where the conventions of behaviour are usually comparatively relaxed and it is easier to introduce incongruity and have fun. In the picture on the right, for example, the curious arrangement was probably arrived at by accident, but it adds a pleasing quality of strangeness without detracting from the art.

Left Decorative objects like these stocking stretchers are not strictly pictures, but they show how many ways there are to animate a wall, making patterns of different shapes.

Right In this room, life is in a state of flux and nothing is what it seems. The ceiling is an important but often neglected face of the six-sided box that forms a room, but here Star Trek figures may use it as their means of entry.

Previous page Spotty pottery and dotty pictures: just seed packets and postcards, but the result is a rich visual feast pinned up along the edge of a kitchen shelf.

Right No picture present, but an assemblage of things in which the frame sets up an expectation of the absent picture. Each element adds something to the totality, whereas individually they would have had no special significance.

Left Simple but seemingly disconnected images nag in the mind, demanding to be made sense of with a logical linkage. This is an extreme form of the challenge presented by most groups of pictures.

SURPRISING PRIZES

The element of surprise begins when you let into your life some object that, like a medieval jester, has the ability both to amuse and to disturb you. It may be a proper work of art, for indeed many works aim for just such an effect, or it may be some other object. It is exhilarating to succumb to buying a painting or print that speaks to you, even though it is quite unlike anything you have ever owned before. Openness to such impulses distinguishes a truly inspired collector from a careful 'amasser of stuff' and requires no greater financial resources.

Your prize (or surprise) may be a chance find, like a photograph, postcard or page taken from a magazine, which may stay temporarily in the home or may take up more permanent residence. Don't let this new image rule your life, but at the same time, don't rule it into submission and silence. Beware, however, of overdoing the simply amusing incongruity: despite the superficial parallels, the jester and the saloon-bar bore are very different creatures.

The jokes can vary between the continuously running variety act and the punch-line. Watching the Disney film *Beauty and the Beast*, for example, we happily go along with the fantasy that the household objects like teapots and candlesticks, which have fallen under the same spell of bewitchment as the Beast, are distinct personalities, interacting with each other. In the same way we can have preferences for certain things that seem to derive from a similar sense of identification.

This may have little to do with the object's functionality or with social convention, even though design historians and museums are not willing to value art by any other yardstick.

The illustrations in this chapter show a variety of surprises. Some are achieved directly through the nature of the objects themselves, others arise from an unexpected positioning, or some slight quality of dislocation, making a reference to their surroundings, intentional or not.

To create the desired spontaneous look, be aware of the way the sun enters a room and where it falls, producing effects of shadow and movement. Then reinforce the echoes that usually arise from any assembly of things. Finally, think about what a room needs to complete it, as the English painter Ben Nicholson did in response to a room just furnished in the early 1930s by his neighbour, the critic Herbert Read – Nicholson popped home returning with a circular cork tablemat, painted bright red, which he nailed off-centre somewhere up near the ceiling.

Zen Buddhists seek understanding through impossible riddles, often seemingly of the simplest kind. Their tradition has influenced many twentieth-century artists, extending their appreciation of art's ability to engage with the world. For followers of Zen, Ben Nicholson's sudden and intuitive response would indicate a man of wisdom. For them, the element of surprise is not the last chapter in the book, but the first.

Left This interior with its newly made structural frame of traditional green oak belongs to the present as well as to the past. The bold print of still life and birds that hangs above the opening to the kitchen relates to the activities below as well as to the two stuffed ducks. 'Skying' pictures like this is not normally considered good practice, but here it seems perfectly natural, both thematically and spatially.

Left The long continuous shelf and walls above the desk and cupboard units offer a perfect stage for a variety of pictures and decorative objects, differing in scale, date and medium. The surprise comes from the shadows cast on the floor, through the glass table top, giving an unexpected view on the world.

TROMPE L'OEIL

MURALS AND

Painting directly on the walls, in the form of murals or painted decoration, is an ancient practice that has largely been replaced by framed movable pictures. There is a special pleasure in being in a room with a painted scheme adapted to the space and the personality of the owner, as seen in the site-specific dining room mural below.

Even amateur artists can have fun painting murals if they work within their technical limitations. Although conceptually simple, the dining room mural below would be difficult to carry out with the machine-like regularity that it requires. On the other hand, there are many examples of folk art painted decoration that have a completely modern kind of freshness and spontaneity and have inspired contemporary decorators from time to time.

Some murals aim specifically to deceive the viewer into seeing spaces and objects that are not there. Called *trompe l'oeil*, they seldom trick the eye for long, but they can be the vehicle for symbolism or poetic fantasy.

Walls may also be papered with prints, with or without their frames, to create a mural effect. Maps, contemporary or historic, look good when pasted on the wall, especially in an entrance hall, or even on a bedroom ceiling for making imaginary journeys at night.

Left These target-like rings are evidently designed for the room, while at the same time pretending to ignore the presence of the Victorian fireplace. This is a skilful yet also rather unsettling scheme of painted decoration.

Right Illusionistic wall painting seldom displays the wit and skill seen in this bathroom, where fragments of ancient Roman architecture and sculpture are painted on real plaster panels, casting their painted shadows onto the walls from left to right, while the real light comes from the right, revealing their pretence.

Left Print rooms, with prints stuck to the wall and framed by paper borders and ornaments, were a popular style of decoration in the eighteenth century. The effect is easy to reconstruct, and original or reproduction prints are not difficult to find. Painted flowerpots in the dado add to the delicate effect.

Below A startling juxtaposition of photographic realism and loose Expressionist painting. The car in the desert looks like a billboard poster and may indeed be one, imposing its giant scale in a relatively small space.

PRACTICALITIES

Museums, collectors and dealers have become increasingly aware of the importance of conservation. It is a fascinating subject, and museum exhibitions devoted to the conservation of an individual work can prove hugely revealing of the artist's intentions and techniques.

For the private collector, there are some simple principles to follow. Do not attempt any cleaning on your own – a dealer in older pictures, a local museum or a well-qualified picture framer can usually put you in touch with a conservator with the appropriate skills.

Oil paintings on canvas are generally more robust than watercolours and other works on paper, but will still benefit from the attention of a professional. Watch out for a loose paint surface, a sagging canvas or any signs of decay on the back. Problems are likely to arise as much from previous botched attempts at restoration as from the deterioration of the original work, so when buying investigate any potential purchases closely. Look out in particular for evidence of overpainting or other interference. One can usually get an instinctive feeling about whether or not a painting feels right for its period.

Above This watercolour by J.M.W. Turner (1775–1851) was given to the British Museum, London, by a private collector. The deed of gift required that it be kept in its specially made frame with a green silk roller blind, fitted by the original owner to preserve the colours.

Below Salvaging pictures during the devastating floods that hit Florence in 1966, when the river Arno burst its banks. Many works in churches and galleries required substantial restoration, and new techniques were evolved to deal with the problems that arose.

Left A paper conservator patiently removes discoloured adhesive from the surface of a red chalk drawing of a male nude. Works on paper can respond almost miraculously to the conservator's skills. After treatment they should be stored and displayed with great care to avoid any further deterioration.

Works on paper are most likely to suffer from the effects of surface dirt, physical damage, damp conditions and acidic mounts, which cause discoloration and staining. Paper can also become creased and need pressing. These problems can be overcome, often quite dramatically, by professional conservators, and it is satisfying to feel that one has contributed to rescuing something valuable from the past.

Much preventive conservation is common sense. Light is the primary enemy, especially of works on paper. This does not mean they have to be kept in the dark, but it is important to avoid direct sunlight. Invest in suitable blinds or curtains so that the works can be protected from the strongest effects of light. In addition, most rooms have darker corners, or parts higher up on the wall where the light does not fall directly, and these can be chosen for hanging more sensitive works.

Watercolour has a reputation as a 'fugitive' medium, meaning that some of the pigments, old or new, can fade over time. Prints with coloured inks and photographs also suffer from fading, and light can damage the paper support as well as the pigment. It is possible to protect precious works by hanging covers over them, displaying them in rotation, using blinds, or, perhaps best of all, covering with an ultra-violet filter glass. It is important with all pictures, however, to strike a balance between protection and enjoyment.

MAKING MOUNTS

A mount is a thin support for a picture, usually a work on paper. A window mount conceals the edges of the picture with a cut-out window overlaid on top. This window opening is usually cut with a sloping angle to smooth the transition between mount and picture. Cutting a mount is a skilled job as flaws tend to be visible. However, with practice and a methodical approach, it is not too difficult to learn the techniques needed. Do make a plan of all dimensions to avoid mistakes!

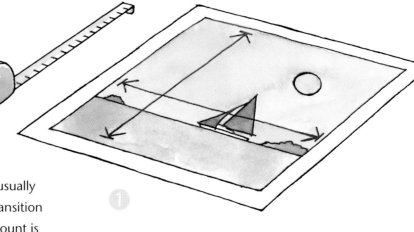

▲ First measure the part of the picture you wish to see inside the window mount, leaving a margin inside the picture of at least 5mm (¼in) all round, then move the picture safely out of the way.

◄ When you have these dimensions, add about 65mm (2½in) around each side of the picture for the mount's border, including an extra 5mm (¼in) to this border at the bottom for visual balance. It can be helpful to make a plan on paper to ensure you have the correct dimensions. Draw the final outside dimensions for your mount in pencil on the back of a piece of mounting board and place this on your cutting surface. Then line up your metal rule with the pencil line and clamp together.

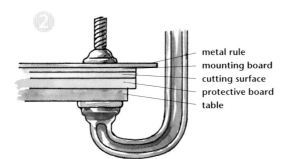

metal rule
mounting board
cutting surface
protective board
table

► With the clamp holding the area you wish to retain, make a gentle cut with your knife, then repeat until the waste board is separated. Repeat for the second side of your mount, using a set square to ensure a right angle at the corner. Now place your finished board face down on a clean work surface, and draw your window on it with a pencil and ruler, measuring in from the edge of the finished board – double check these inside dimensions by laying the picture on top.

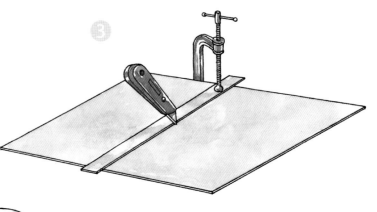

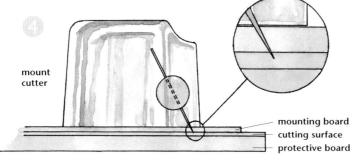

mount cutter

mounting board
cutting surface
protective board

◄ You are now ready to cut your window in the mounting board using a mount cutter. Remember to adjust the blade of the mount cutter to the thickness of the mounting board you are using. You can first test the blade against an offcut: it should cut into the cutting surface beneath, but not right through it.

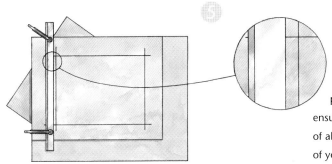

◄ Clamp your mounting board, cutting surface and protective board to the table with the metal rule on top as before – placing them diagonally on the table can ensure a good grip. Remember to leave a gap of about 5mm (¼in) between the straight edge of your metal rule and the pencil line to allow for the offset of the mount cutter's blade.

Positioning the metal rule
To find the width of the gap required to allow for the offset of the mount cutter's blade, test on an offcut first, and create a card 'spacer'. This will allow you to place the metal rule correctly each time.

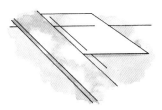

► Insert the point of the blade at an intersection of the pencil lines, pressing it gently into the mounting board, and then set off, pushing along the edge of the metal rule. After the first cut, unclamp the rule and turn the mounting board over to check the depth of the cut, adjust the blade if necessary, and repeat along each side. At corners, remember to push the blade so that its back edge lines up with the intersection of the pencil lines – this should ensure a clean cut.

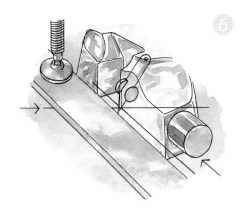

On the final cut
Before you reach the last corner, lay a thin piece of scrap paper under the mount cutter to prevent it catching on the original cut.

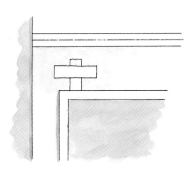

►▼ The centre of the mount should now drop out, although it may still need some delicate work with a scalpel at the corners. Next cut a piece of plain board to the same size as the mount and create a hinge between the two with a length of gummed linen tape.

Attaching the boards together
Attach the back of your window to a piece of board with linen tape, and trim at the edges, leaving the front of the mount pristine.

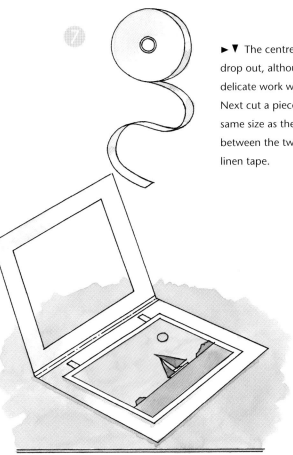

BACK

Attaching tabs to the picture
Turn the picture round and fix two short tabs of linen tape to the top of the picture's back, taking care not to wet the tape too much. Then place in the mount and close the front to check the picture's position.

Sticking the picture to the mount
When you are satisfied with the placement of the picture in the mount, stick it in place using more linen tape, and then close your mount. Gummed tape is easily removable if you change your mind later.

FRAMES

MAKING

The theory of frame-making is relatively simple, but in practice it can prove rather more complex. Only the basic tools and techniques are discussed here. Frame mouldings, from which the frame is made, are available in many shapes, finishes and materials, but unpainted wood is probably the best to begin with. These mouldings incorporate a 'rebate' (see right) at the back into which your picture will fit. The first step in framing is to check that the picture you wish to frame is square. To do this, check the two diagonal measurements from corner to corner. If they are not equal, you will need to choose a moulding with a rebate wide enough to conceal the problem.

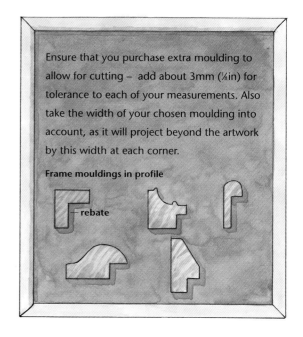

Ensure that you purchase extra moulding to allow for cutting – add about 3mm (⅛in) for tolerance to each of your measurements. Also take the width of your chosen moulding into account, as it will project beyond the artwork by this width at each corner.

Frame mouldings in profile

rebate

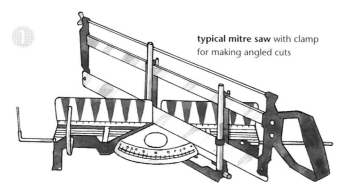

typical **mitre saw** with clamp for making angled cuts

▶ Measure out the length of the first side of the picture on the moulding, including an extra 3mm (⅛in) to prevent too tight a fit in the finished frame. Mark the next cut in pencil at this point, check against the picture, and cut the moulding at this point with the mitre saw as before.

◀ **Cutting the moulding** Take one piece of moulding and make a mitre cut – a 45° angle cut – at one end: for best results use a combined saw and clamp like the one illustrated here. Saw slowly, letting the weight of the saw do the cutting rather than forcing the blade down and damaging the wood.

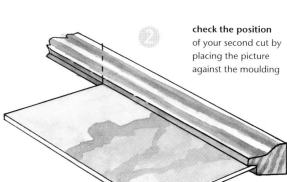

check the position of your second cut by placing the picture against the moulding

◀ Once you have cut the first length of moulding, make a mitre cut at the end of the new piece, hold the first piece alongside and use as a guide for the length of this second piece. Cut with the mitre saw, and then repeat the procedure for the third and fourth pieces.

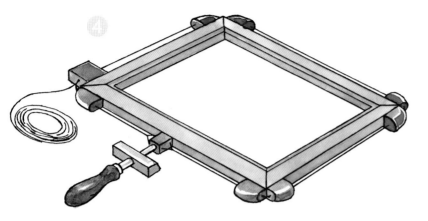

◀ **Fixing the frame** The mitre saw is often sold in a package with a frame clamp, like the one shown here, with a frame inside (left). It holds all the corners in place with a firm, even pressure while the glue dries. Any excess glue that oozes from the joint while clamping is in progress should always be wiped away immediately. Each corner should also be pinned afterwards for additional strength, with panel pins about twice as long as the width of the moulding.

▶ Insert the panel pins at the top and bottom of the frame where they are unlikely to be visible. Drill or spike a hole, slightly smaller in diameter than your pin, into the frame first to prevent the ends of the moulding splitting. Drive the pins into the frame with a tack hammer (right), inserting them at a slight angle to each other to help them achieve purchase at the join. Then push them below the surface of the frame using a nail punch (left). Finally fill the resulting holes with woodfiller and cover with spots of paint applied with a fine brush.

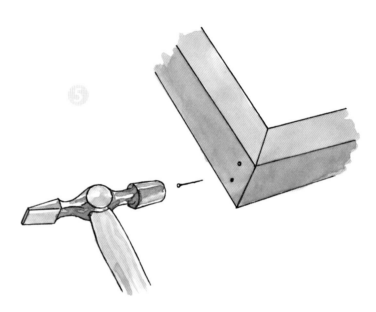

A typical 'sandwich'

- glass
- mount and backing
- hardboard
- pin

◀ **Fixing the artwork** Sand away any rough areas of unpainted wood and fill any holes in the frame – you can apply a stained or painted finish on the frame at this point to suit the artwork, even using gold leaf if you are ambitious! Then gently lay the frame front-side down on a soft surface. Clean your glass carefully on both sides (a supplier should be happy to cut glass to your specifications) and then lay it carefully into the rebate of the frame.

▶ Next place your artwork, mounted or otherwise, face down over the glass, and finally insert a piece of hardboard backing cut to size. Check that there are no specks trapped inside the picture before you fix the sandwich in place. It is possible to purchase a 'point gun' to secure the artwork, but a series of pins inserted with a hammer into the frame's rebate, tight up against the backing board, should do the job. Finally seal up the joins between the frame and the hardboard all around with lengths of gummed paper tape.

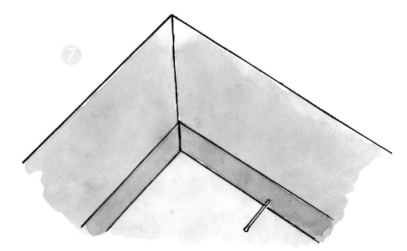

TYPES OF FRAME

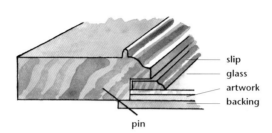

slip
glass
artwork
backing
pin

◄ **Slip** A slip is often inserted between a frame and the glass as an additional decorative surround. It can be treated with a colour that blends or contrasts with the rest of the frame or can be covered with a fabric such as hessian. Slips are readily available in a variety of finishes, and should be cut with mitred ends to fit the outer frame. If you are careful they fit snugly without any need for gluing. When the resulting 'sandwich' exceeds the depth of the frame's rebate, a slightly larger backing will be needed, which can be fastened with pins driven diagonally into the frame (see left).

► Slips can also be placed in between the glass and the backing to frame a picture in low relief or with projecting areas, such as a collage or a painting with thick *impasto*. Any suitable wooden moulding can be used for a slip, and altered as required.

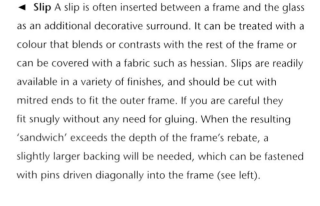

glass
slip
artwork on mount
backing

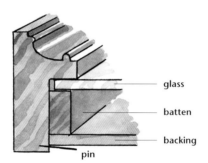

glass
batten
backing
pin

◄ **Box frames** If you wish to display bulky items such as medals, jewellery, or even wooden carvings, behind glass, you will need a frame with a deep rebate. A thin piece of wood called a batten can be concealed in the frame to separate the glass and the backing board. Again, if carefully cut, no gluing or pinning of the battens should be necessary to hold them in place.

► **Double glass frames** If your artwork has something interesting on the reverse, you can choose a moulding with a deep rebate to accommodate two layers of glass. Use glass at least 3mm (⅛in) thick for the back layer to prevent cracking. Fix this sandwich in place with lengths of slip moulding pinned around the back of the frame. Alternatively, you can sandwich two pieces of glass together with masking tape and place in a frame with turn buttons (see p.137) without any backing board, thus allowing both sides of the artwork to be seen with comparitive ease.

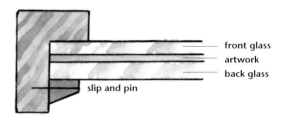

front glass
artwork
back glass
slip and pin

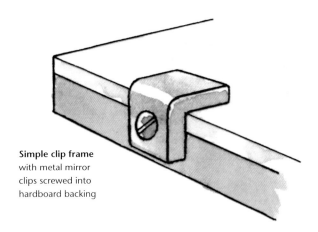

Simple clip frame
with metal mirror
clips screwed into
hardboard backing

◄ **Removable backs** Most frames are relatively hard to take apart. If you are likely to change your pictures around in their frames frequently, you may wish to consider using clip frames. These are ideal for posters and prints, but are less suitable for anything that might be damaged by dust. Most have a hardboard backing, and simple metal or plastic 'mirror clips', screwed to the edge of the backing with chipboard screws. It is usually better to use acetate rather than glass, as the latter can shatter under the pressure of the mirror clips.

► Frames are also available with 'turn buttons' (right) which are screwed to the back of the frame, and can be twisted to allow for the removal of artwork and backing board. As with more traditional frames, it is generally a good idea to mount the artwork or poster on card to protect it from any unevenness in the hardboard backing.

Turn buttons
made of brass screwed
to a simple frame

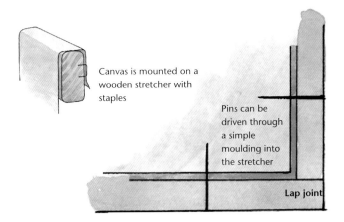

Canvas is mounted on a
wooden stretcher with
staples

Pins can be
driven through
a simple
moulding into
the stretcher

Lap joint

◄ **A simple frame** Oil paintings on canvas are usually mounted on wooden stretchers, with the canvas fixed to the stretcher at the back with staples. A simple frame can thus be made by attaching a narrow moulding directly to this stretcher with pins that go through the moulding and into the stretcher (left). If you do not have a mitre saw, 'lap' joints, where one piece of wood abuts the other at a right angle at the corner of the frame, can look elegant, particularly on modern works. But beware canvases that are not square!

► **A modern frame** The English painter Ben Nicholson (1894–1982) liked to frame his abstract paintings and reliefs with a special lap joint at the corner in place of a mitre joint. Each length of moulding would overlap at the corner with the next in a rotational sequence, creating what is known as a 'chase-me-charlie' joint.

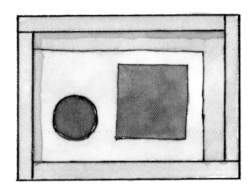

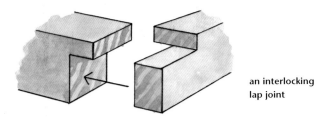

**an interlocking
lap joint**

◄ It is necessary to choose a flat-topped moulding for this frame. You will need to saw the interlocking lap joint at the end of the moulding very carefully, as the ends split easily, and a good fit with the artwork is important.

AND DISPLAYING

HANGING

Having chosen your approach to displaying your pictures, it is important not to overlook the practical aspects of hanging – your picture must not fall off the wall if you can possibly help it. It is also vital to keep an eye on your pictures once hung. Check older frames periodically to ensure that the cord and hooks are still strong enough. The glass on glazed pictures will need regular cleaning, using a minimal amount of moisture to ensure dampness does not penetrate the frame.

Plug

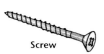

Screw

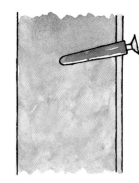

◀ For hard walls (concrete, brick, or cement under a thin skin of plaster), you will need to drill a hole, and then fix the screw with a plug, leaving about 3mm (⅛in) projecting.

◀ For lighter pictures on soft walls such as plasterboard and soft plaster, a hook and nail such as this is the easiest solution.

◀ Double and triple versions of such hooks are also available, which help to spread the load of a picture over a wider area of wall.

◀ Multiple pin hooks such as this are now readily available, and are particularly appropriate for a attaching to a thin layer of plaster.

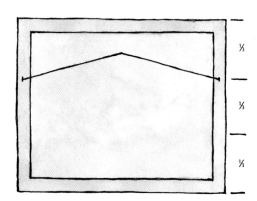

⅓

⅓

⅓

◀ **Lighter pictures** Position the hooks (known as screw eyes) about a third of the way down the frame, having first made pilot holes with a thin drill bit or spike. Then stretch brass wire or nylon cord through them at double thickness and tie, allowing a little slack. Make sure the cord will not show above the frame once the work has been hung. For narrow mouldings, where the hook might split the wood, D-rings which fit into the backing board are also available, and have the advantage of remaining hidden. Remember to fit them to the hardboard before assembling the frame.

Mirror plate

front   **back**

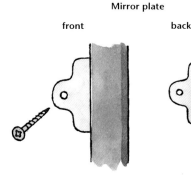

▶ **Heavier pictures** For large or heavy works, the best option is probably to hang them using mirror plates (right). These allow the work to sit flush against the wall, and can be fixed at the top edge or at both sides with brass screws. Always use wall plugs for particularly heavy frames. Concealed mirror plates are also available but can prove awkward to attach to the wall. You could also consider a gallery-type hanging system (see p.104) with sturdy rails at the top of the wall or behind the pictures.

◄ **Positioning on the wall** First hold the picture against the wall to check its position, or better get someone else to hold it up, allowing you to stand back and gauge how it looks in its surroundings.

► When you are happy with the position, find the 'fixing point' on the wall by placing one hand between the wall and the painting, and pushing up the centre of the cord. Remove the picture with the other hand, and mark this fixing point by a small 'x' in pencil on the wall – for large pictures two people may be necessary to achieve this with ease.

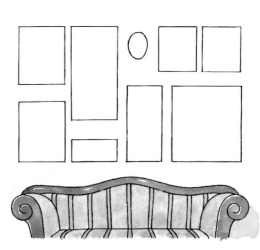

◄ **Fixing the hook** Remember that your 'x' marking the fixing point is the position for the base of the hook, not for the nail itself. The picture's cord will probably sag over a period of time. If you find the picture has become too low, the best solution is probably to remove the painting and tighten its cord rather than move the hook.

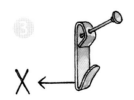

It is important to establish an outer limit to the group of pictures you wish to display – this will often relate to nearby furniture, lighting and curtains.

◄▲ **Planning a group of pictures** Try laying out your selection of pictures together on the floor and experimenting with different combinations. To gauge their final effect before making holes in the wall, you can cut pieces of paper to the same sizes as your pictures and attach them to the wall in your chosen arrangement.

INDEX

AUTHOR'S ACKNOWLEDGMENTS
I am grateful to all the members of the publishing team who have worked so harmoniously to produce this book, and to my wife Susanna for support at home. My thanks are also due to Greville Rhodes who taught me how to frame pictures many years ago.

PHOTO ACKNOWLEDGMENTS
The publisher would like to thank the following for their kind permission to reproduce photographs in this book

Front cover Int/Corinne Calesso; **Back cover, l** EWA; **Back cover, r** IA/HW/Giola Rossi; **Endpapers** Paul Rocheleau/Arquitectonica/Spear House; **1** EWA; **2** IA/HW; **5** IA/Andrew Wood/Artist: Kitty North; **6 t** National Gallery, London; **6 b** AKG, London/Kunsthistorisches Museum/Erich Lessing; **7** National Gallery, London; **8** Architect's Journal; **9** Bridgeman Art Library/Linley Sambourne House, London, UK; **10–11** Axiom Photographic Agency/Luke White; **12** Abode; **13** IA/Simon Brown/Artist: Rebecca Hossack; **14 t** Arcaid/ Alan Weintraub; **14 b** Ma; **15** Ma; **16** Ma; **17** H&I/Verne; **18** Ma; **19** Ma; **20 t** EWA/Spike Powell; **20 b** Int/Designer: Jan des Bouvrie; **21** Arcaid/Alan Weintraub; **22** IA/Simon Brown/Conran; **23** Ma; **24** Richard Glover/Arthur Collin Architect; **26** Arcaid/ Alan Weintraub; **27** IA/Edina van der Wyck; **28** IA/Edina van der Wyck/Jenny Armit; **29 l** IA/Andrew Wood; **29 r** IA/Andrew Wood; **30** IA/Tim Beddow/Emma Fole; **31** William R Tingey; **33 t** Bridgeman Art Library/Château de Versailles, France/Giraudon; **33 b** AKG, London; **34** EWA/Mark Lufcombe White; **34 t** Curwen Chilford Prints Ltd; **34 b** Victoria & Albert Museum, London; **36 t** Abode; **36 b** Ma; **37** EWA/Andreas v. Einseidel; **38 t** Aix-en-Provence Office of Tourism; **38 b** RD; **39** IA/Jacques Dirand; **40** RD; **41 t** RD; **41 b** IA/Simon Upton/Designers: Marja Walters/Michael Reeves; **42** EWA/Rodney Hyett; **43** Arcaid/Richard Waite/ Jane Collins; **44–5** RD; **46** H&I/Verne; **47 r** IA/Andrew Wood/Designer: Stephanie Hoppen; **48 t** Ma; **48 b** Ma; **49** RD/Thanks to David Gentleman; **50** Richard Glover/Architect: John Pawson; **52** View/Peter Cook; **53 t** IA/HW/Architect: Helen St Cyr; **53 b** IA/ Edina van der Wyck/Ehrhardt; **54** Richard Glover/Architect: John Pawson; **55 t** EWA/Tim Street Porter; **55 b** Axiom Photographic Agency/James Morris/Architect: Will White; **56 t** Axiom Photographic Agency/James Morris/Pip Horne; **56 b** Ma; **58–9** Paul Rocheleau/Johnson/Johnson; **60** Arcaid/Georgie Cole/Belle; **61 t** Int/Designer: Kim Heirston; **61 b** Arcaid/Earl Carter/Belle; **62** Artsway/photo Gina Deardon; **63 t** New Art Centre/photo by Joe Low/Thanks to Paul Huxley; **63 b** Ma; **64** RD; **66** Arcaid/Alan Weintraub; **67** IA/Andrew Wood/Designer Stephen Bayley; **68** H&I/Simon Butcher; **69** Ma; **70** RD; **71** H&I/Verne; **72** Int/Designer: Corinne Calesso; **73** IA/Fritz von der Sculenburg/Designer: Cath Kidston; **74** Mainstream/V Wolf; **75** IA/Simon Upton/Bill Amberg; **76** H&I/Verne; **77** Int/Thanks to Gilbert & George; **78–9** View/Peter Cook; **80** Int/Designer: Chuck & Martha Baker; **81 t** Ma; **81 b** IA/HW/Peter Hinwood; **82 l** IA/HW/Giola Rossi; **83** Ma; **84 t** Abode; **84 b** EWA; **85** Abode; **86** View/Peter Cook/Priest's House, restored by Architecton; **88** Ma; **89 t** Ma; **89 b** EWA/Tim Street Porter; **90** View/Peter Cook; **91** Ma/Eltham Palace; **92** IA/ Christopher Simon Sykes; **93** William R Tingey; **94** Ma; **96** IA/Andrew Wood; **97 l** IA/Simon Upton; **97 r** IA/HW/Architect: Voon Vee Vong; **98 b** Ma; **99** Ma; **99 r** IA/Simon Upton/Owner: Anita Jenkins; **99 b** Ma; **100** Ma; **102 l** IA/Simon Upton/Designer: Ann Boyd; **103** National Trust Photographic Library/Geoffrey Frosh; **104** Int/Designer: Christian Liaigre; **105 t** Ma; **105 b** Abode; **106** IA/ Christopher Simon Sykes/Owner: Fred Hughes; **107** IA/HW/Designer: Emma Kennedy; **108** Int; **110** EWA; **111 l** IA/Jacques Dirand; **111 r** IA/HW/Antonio; **112 t** RD/Thanks to Howard Hodgkin; **112 b** Arcaid/Jeremy Cockayne; **113 l** EWA/Peter Wolosynski; **113 r** Arcaid/Richard Bryant; **114** RD; **116** RD; **117** Ma; **118 t** Ma; **118 b** IA/Edina van der Wyck; **119** H&I/Verne; **120** Ma; **122** Arcaid/Alan Weintraub; **123** Ma; **124** View/Philip Bier; **125** Arcaid/Alan Weintraub; **126 l** Ma; **126 r** IA/Jacques Dirand/ Ricardo Cinalli; **127 t** National Trust Photographic Library/Geoffrey Frosh; **127 b** Ma; **128–9** View/Dennis Gilbert; **130 t** British Museum, London; **130 b** CatPress, Florence; **131** Sophia Fairclough & Suzy Watters Ltd; **132–9** artwork ©OPG/by David Ashby

Key t top, b bottom, l left, r right
EWA Elizabeth Whiting Associates; H&I Houses & Interiors; HW Henry Wilson; IA The Interior Archive;
Int International Interiors/Paul Ryan; Ma Mainstream/Ray Main; RD Richard Davies